Long Haul LEGACY

SMC³

Publisher: Atlanta Book Printing
(dba Premier Graphics & Communications)
Jacket Design: Andrew Harmon Design
Book Layout and Design: Gary G. Pulliam

Photo Section Credits: Associated Press,
Michael Gibson, Lee Cathey, Getty Images,
Dollar Photo Club, and SMC³ owned

Copyright © F. Martin Harmon.

All rights reserved. No part of this book may be reproduced in any form or by any means without prior written permission from the author, except for brief quotations used in reviews written specifically for inclusion in a magazine, newspaper, or for broadcast media.

Printed in the United States of America
First Printing, 2015 • Atlanta, Georgia

ISBN: 978-1-68026-023-6
Library of Congress: 2015950228

www.smc3.com | www.fmartinharmon.com

Table of Contents

Introduction – The First 80 Years v

Chapter 1 – Shared Success Story 1

Chapter 2 – How Trucking Kept 'em On The Farm............. 7

Chapter 3 – Regulation and Collective Ratemaking.......... 13

Chapter 4 – The Interstate Transformation....................... 21

Chapter 5 – Looking Back at Bureau Days 27

Chapter 6 – Of Zip Codes and Benchmarks 35

Chapter 7 – Surviving Identity 43

Chapter 8 – Labor Pains of Merger 51

Chapter 9 – Regulation Reminiscing................................... 57

Chapter 10 – "Intimidating Times" 67

Chapter 11 – "Values Driven" Trilogy 73

Chapter 12 – Of Rates and The Cloud................................. 81

Chapter 13 – New Age, New Leadership............................. 89

Postscript 93

Appendixes...97-100

Chapter Notes.. 101

Selected Bibliography 109

Acknowledgements 115

Index 117

Introduction:
The First 80 Years

To say it's an unlikely story would be an understatement. To downplay its importance in the modern transportation marketplace would diminish what has become an American way of life, and to overlook the success it has enjoyed despite decades of crossroads is to miss a key component in the evolution of North American motor freight. This is the story of Southern Motor Carriers, what was originally known as Southern Motor Carriers Rate Conference or SMCRC and most recently (in the latest century) as SMC³. However, it's about much more than that. Not a well-known brand like IBM or AT&T outside the industry, it's nevertheless enjoyed a similarly influential role in the development of this country over the last 80 years.

One has only to take a drive on the multi-lane freeways of this land to understand this influence. Ever count the 18-wheelers you encounter between home and any out-of-town destination? Or better yet, just take a spin around the expressways of any major American city – "The Perimeter" around Atlanta, "The Beltway" that encircles D.C., or "The Tom Landry Freeway" between Dallas and Fort Worth just to name a few – and your appreciation for this organization, this 501(c)(6) nonprofit, tax exempt trade association, should grow. Just count the trucks . . . and I mean the big, diesel trucks you must constantly maneuver around and through. Most are moving freight courtesy of the system and service provided by this little known acronym (at least outside the industry) in Peachtree City, Georgia. Without

SMC³, what it did and now does, chaos might reign up and down the American supply chain - or at the very least it would reign if somebody else, by this time, had not accomplished what SMC³ accomplished and has become.

Just as our dependence on computers and technology, and every piece of data that so seamlessly flows through our nationwide hard drives, is alarmingly apparent every day (especially so when there's a major internet security breech), so too the technology of SMC³ has played a leading role in the where-we-are-now world of motor freight. It's a story driven by trucks and the companies (or carriers) who run those trucks, as well as the shippers who manufacture, develop, and at least ensure there's always something to put on those trucks. It's a story tied to the history of transportation in this country, for better or worse, good times and bad, no matter what turns it has taken or where it has led. Included in its chapters are courtrooms and congressional chambers, lawsuits and mergers, more government intervention and much less. It's got a language and terminology all its own that doesn't include 10-4 good buddy or got your ears on. No, for all of its connection to that mythic American pioneer known as the truck driver, a time-honored workforce now in too short supply, it's much more complex and far reaching.

After all, it's all about rates; those prices for services rendered whenever a carrier loads his truck with a shipper's goods and transports it from point A to point B, and quite possibly lots of points in between. The what, where, and why of those rates is a huge part of this story, but there's a myriad of other factors that have always entered in as well and that includes the who and how in this integral piece of the puzzle. Originally compiled and called tariffs (and not the import kind often referred to in American History 101), these published rates were the early bedrock of the industry on a regional basis when government was much more involved than it is today. Learn how it was done then and now. Learn about the creation of the CzarLite family of rate computing software that modernized motor freight pricing, and how zip codes again solved transportation issues long after they came into existence as the postal service's "zone improvement plan" in 1963.

Chapter 1 begins with the two men most responsible for this story. It moves on to organizational beginnings by representatives of nine southern states in the collective transportation atmosphere of the 1930s; it encompasses the original concept, articles of incorporation, and actual resolution it was created from; and it touches on the impending national drama of deregulation, something that officially occurred in 1980, but a misnomer according to outgoing SMC³ CEO Jack Middleton since that process actually lasted all the way through December 31, 2008. See how a series of episodes were required, both by the industry and SMC³, to weather this storm and ultimately survive when much else of 20th Century motor freight was rapidly changing.

Flashing back in Chapters 2 through 5, learn how trucking got its start in this country in the early 1900s; how governmental regulation in the mid-1900s imposed boundaries, routes, and regional partnerships while also ushering in unionization and consolidation, trends that have always had a role while at the same time exacting a toll. Learn about the rates and the data that went into formulating them, and how the massive Interstate Highway System dramatically affected the future of motor freight in the mid to late 1900s while imposing much needed infrastructure into our present and beyond. This early industry history created the environment that led to the start of SMC³ in the 1930s along with other regional rate bureaus, a process that worked well amidst industry regulation, but a system that was quickly outdated and unsustainable once deregulation commenced with two decades left in the last century.

Into this new era of intense competition, see how SMC³ adapted in Chapters 6 through 8 while most of the other bureaus were gradually going out of business – what one longtime SMC³ Board member recently termed, "survival of the fittest" - and how, exactly, that happened. Learn the intricate and often contentious steps that were necessary to convert this printer-based, collective rates publishing provider into the dynamic, forward-thinking, and essential association that it is today. Gain an understanding of the original CZAR technology that re-shaped the industry during the late 1980s, as well as how it all came about.

Learn in Chapters 9 and 10 about the tense times that motor freight faced in the final two decades of the last century and through at least seven years of the present one. Understand how the end of antitrust, the departure from states' rights, and SMC³'s push for nationwide authority shaped the modern transportation landscape, and in Chapter 11, examine how industry education became an integral part of SMC³'s new trilogy mission of technology, data, and education. With twice annual conferences and prominent panels now attracting between 300 and 400 carriers, shippers, and logistic professionals each time, and with regular industry-related seminars sponsored each year, you are made aware of SMC³'s ongoing commitment to its members, customers, partners, and constituents. In Chapter 12, explore the extreme difference between truckload ratemaking and less than truckload, and the ongoing technological advances SMC³ is making for the industry's betterment. And finally in Chapter 13, explore industry academic trends and what SMC³ is already addressing in order to maintain its hard-won viability into the future under new president Andrew Slusher.

In telling this tale, SMC³'s history is rendered synonymous with the story of motor freight in this country. Or, more appropriately, the evolution of motor freight, which rolls on despite ongoing traffic and safety concerns, infrastructure problems, the new challenges posed by e-commerce, and the dawn of dimensional pricing, as well as a lack of both capacity and drivers in the immediate future. No longer just an LTL service provider as truckload tendencies already loom greater on the horizon and 3PLs increasingly join shippers and carriers in its industry (and client) makeup, SMC³ must remain vigilant and inclusive of all supply chains and logistics as it seeks to remain the industry's technology, data, and educational leader for another 80 years and beyond.

Long Haul LEGACY

F. Martin Harmon

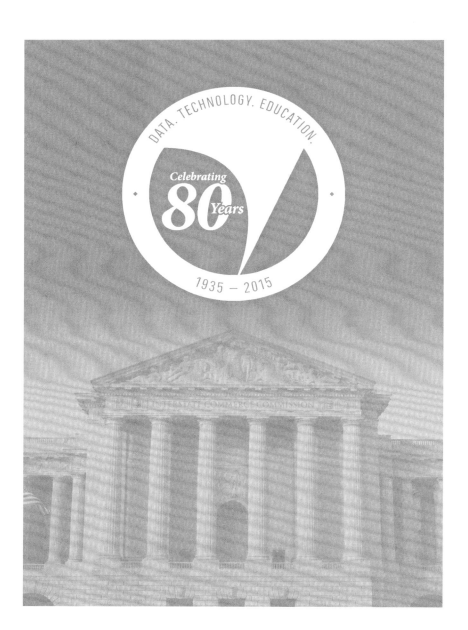

Chapter one
Shared Success Story

Two men, one the embattled survivor of a bygone age of trucking regulation and the other a master strategist who positioned the organization for success in the midst of deregulating transition — together they shaped the inspiring legacy that is SMC³. The preservation battle they waged is the real story of SMC³ today, the story of how one of the original trucking rate bureaus continued when most others were forced to shutter their doors. Thanks to them, their loyal governing boards, and dedicated staffs, Atlanta-based SMC³ not only survived, but prospered, even when the odds seemed stacked against it numerous times.

Theirs is the real story here, the story that coincides with the evolution of motor freight in this country. Because of them this story could be written. Because of them this story deserves to be told and shared with others in the transportation world, both now and in the future. Because of the two of them, the American supply chain is better.

At its most critical junctures, this eight decades-old tale is the story of Vernon Farriba and Jack Middleton, two leaders with determination and vision who never considered the meaning of can't in their collective quest to ensure the existence and heritage of SMC³. Although a little known entity outside the industry, "it's an incredible success story that everyone in the industry should know about," according to John Langley, a much-respected professor of supply chain management at Penn State University.[1] From years and years of living with the threat of extinction through the stressful but very necessary days of litigation and adaptation, Farriba and Middleton shared the torch that illuminated the path to success, not only for SMC³ but for the entire motor freight industry.

* * * * * * *

Establishing the exact moment SMC³ came into existence is hard to do, as various meetings and steps led to its creation, but the reason it came into existence was never in doubt. The Motor Carrier Act of 1935 stimulated a need for collective rate bureaus throughout the country as the suddenly regulated early trucking companies banded together regionally to establish and publish their collective rates in an organized fashion. This was in response to the more chaotic and time-consuming alternative that setting and maintaining their rates individually would have been. With trucking routes in those days confined and based on "economic need," it made sense for individual motor carriers in each area of the country to work together towards the common good, a system that would also be conducive to industry-wide organization.[2]

Such was the regionally collective environment that SMC³ was initially born into and what would remain for the next 45 years. Its stated mission:

> "To encourage and foster a feeling of friendship between those who are engaged in the transportation of property by motor vehicle(s) on the streets and highways of the United States and particularly in the states of Alabama, Florida, Georgia, Louisiana, Mississippi, North Carolina, South Carolina, Tennessee, and Virginia."

More specifically, the SMCRC Articles of Incorporation called for a "spirit of cooperation" in all membership matters of mutual interest; the gathering, tabulating, and disseminating of industry information among members; the improvement of the industry in "every proper and lawful manner;" membership meetings at stated periods "for the discussion of reliable information" related to the best methods of conducting practical and ethical business; and finally, the compilation, publishing, printing, and filing with the Interstate Commerce Commission (ICC) and state regulatory commissions of tariffs and tariff changes "required by law." In addition, it was to advocate for its members in all matters of a regulatory nature.[3]

Documentation points to the offices of the Atlanta Chamber of Commerce and November 27, 1935 for initial confirmation of the developing association,[4] but incorporation of the original Southern Motor Carriers Rate Conference as a non-profit, 501(c)(6) association actually took place in neighboring Florida (still among the top five states in which to incorporate) after seven months of examination on May 31, 1936.[5] There's no doubt early impetus was also provided by the North Carolina Truck Owners Association, which was founded in 1929, one of the first such in-state associations in the South.[6]

According to a speech given by then SMCRC Executive Vice President W. M. (Mike) Miller nearly 30 years later on January 15, 1964, the first organizational meetings for the Southern Motor Carriers Rate Conference were actually held in three different states during the latter part of 1935. Representatives of Georgia's trucking companies met on August 16, those from South Carolina on August 20, and North Carolina representatives got together on August 29, all leading up to a joint meeting of the motor carriers from each of those states on August 30.[7] From those initial meetings, a multi-faceted resolution was passed at a meeting in Asheville, North Carolina on September 9 of that same year, which stated:

> "Resolved: That motor truck rates in the territory east of the Mississippi River and south of the Ohio and Potomac Rivers be based on a uniform simplified classification, compiled by giving consideration to truck requisites, value of commodities, and competition.
>
> Resolved: That the motor truck rates in the territory east of the Mississippi and south of the Ohio and Potomac be established by giving due consideration to the inherent

advantage of such transportation; to the effect of the rates upon the movement of traffic (with relation to existing competition), and to truck operating costs, plus a reasonable profit.

Whereas: The varying weight or load limit laws of the different states have a direct influence on motor truck rates and act as a barrier toward establishing a national or even a sectional uniform tariff, be it resolved that the Interstate Commerce Commission be requested to take immediate steps to ensure uniform weight laws in all states.

Resolved: That there be organized a Southern Motor Carriers Rate Conference composed of three representatives of Virginia, North Carolina, South Carolina, Tennessee, Kentucky, Georgia, Alabama, Mississippi, and Florida to jointly consider rate problems; and that the rate committees in the above states act in this capacity until the various state organizations elect others."[8]

Just over a month later on October 14, all of this was officially adopted at another meeting despite debate as to whether the bureau office should be located in Atlanta or Louisville. In fact, at that same meeting in Chicago, it was decided that both southern cities would have bureaus and the work divided between the two,[9] a development that would lead to ramifications five decades later. The Atlanta office dates to November 1, 1935 and its initial filing of 10 tariffs with the ICC took place in April 1936.

Flashing forward four decades, the mission remained essentially the same, but the environment was very different. Antitrust dictates that had initially been ignored and later condoned[10] when it came to the still developing trucking business were again making the rounds of governmental discussion. Re-affirming and re-opening competition in the laissez-faire inspired American marketplace seemed to be of uppermost importance to congressional minds by the 1980s, no matter the industry or how sustainable it had become.[11] In addition, computerization was cresting the horizon in ever increasing rays of innovative technology, giving rise to new initiatives and ways of doing things that would eventually usher in new approaches and competitions throughout American life. Like all transportation, trucking, and more specifically carrier ratemaking, was no exception.[12]

Bridging this era, Farriba's directorship lasted from early 1976, when he replaced the suddenly dismissed Bill Brown, through 1995, when he recommended Middleton as his successor over initial Board objection due to the fact Middleton's background was from the accounting and personnel side of the equation rather than the tariff (or ratemaking) side, which had always been the leadership path before.[13] Over the next two decades, that would prove a very fortuitous decision and one Farriba proudly remembered when he stated, "Having witnessed Jack's accomplishments in making our Accounting Department state of the art and his handling of our merger with a sister bureau, one of the greatest organizational challenges we ever faced, it was obvious that Jack had to be given every consideration for the CEO position. His organizational skills and ability to recognize and employ skilled people were outstanding, and he possessed the kind of vision that never becomes obsolete."[14]

So the accountant-turned-transportation CEO got his chance to bring Southern Motor Carriers into the new century. For the time being, survival had been assured through carrier loyalty and by ensuring identity through merger and progress into the computer age. The future seemed brighter, but pitfalls still loomed in the form of government intervention and litigation. For the time being, however, business into the future had been maintained and not just regionally - nationally. The rate bureau era was nearing an end, but the business of what would eventually become SMC[3] was just getting started.[15] It all seemed very different, but it was still based on trucking and all to the benefit of American motor freight.

Chapter two

How Trucking Kept 'em On The Farm

There's no disputing the fact that trucking in America and the movement of freight by trucks had its beginnings down on the farm.[16] In fact, the popular song near the end of World War I that posed the question "how you gonna keep 'em down on the farm once they've seen Paree" referenced American soldiers returning from the battlefields of Europe by way of Paris,[17] but it also tied together two origins of trucking in this country – the use of motorized conveyance vehicles to move supplies during the first world war followed by their use to move produce to market once many of those soldiers returned to their rural roots.[18] Although many point to the year 1896 as the introduction of motorized trucking in this country[19] and early automakers like the Autocar Company of Ardmore, Pennsylvania (1897), the Mack Brothers Company of Brooklyn, New York (1900), and Diamond Reo of Chicago, Illinois (1905) introduced larger than normal automobiles,[20] what the *New York Times* labeled "the new mechanical wagon(s)" with their extended wheelbases and rear hauling platforms prior to the conflict,[21] "the war to end wars" accelerated their evolution dramatically. World War I actually caused trucks (many of them with covered platforms) to become integral components of the American military and the new means of hauling, while also inspiring returning farm boys to begin using them as essential movers in the modern supply chains so visible on our highways today.[22]

With thousands of rural-based "Dough Boys" back, the 1920s became years of plenty for U.S. farmers with surpluses that actually began during the war and what Shane Hamilton, in his 2008 book *Trucking Country*, termed, "a golden age of agriculture." Due to the rise of populism in the late 1800s through the political leadership of rural-rousing orators like William Jennings Bryan and an increasing global demand for U.S. farm products, American agrarians became more accomplished advocates of their own interests.[23] As the decade progressed, many were not willing to accept the notion that those same surpluses had to cease in order for their products to remain profitable once the Great Depression began and New Deal regulators began calling for agricultural limits. In other words, produce-less-if-you-want-to-make-more did not make much sense to farmers confronted by the Agricultural Adjustment Act of 1933, which was designed to shore up incomes through price supports and production controls primarily for the benefit (and votes) of American consumers.[24] By that time, more and more produce and livestock were getting to the railroads and their nationwide markets on the beds of trucks, so cutting back didn't seem to make sense, particularly with so many southern and midwestern farm boys driving trucks.

At the same time, refrigerated rail transport (invented in the 1890s) had already done so much to aid milk and meat delivery that moving those essential products had been altered to the point of causing "milk wars" and "beef monopolies."[25] Such confrontations and consolidations further thrust trucking to the forefront of the budding rural crisis, especially when farm boys started looking for alternatives to make a living at the same time they and their families were trying to stay in the country and out of urban factories.

In 1940, Humphrey Bogart and George Raft starred in the movie *They Drive By Night,* the story of two "wildcat truckers" starting out during the depression, the era that spawned this breed.[26] Two of the more successful, real-life examples of that group would be Webb Wallace Estes, of Chase City, Virginia, who turned transporting his neighbors' livestock to market in 1931 into a family-owned, nationwide company recognized coast-to-coast as "Big E," the logo-inspired moniker for Estes Express Lines; and Johnnie Bryan Hunt, the son of Arkansas sharecroppers who, despite a mere seventh grade education, started a vast trucking and intermodal empire (containerized shipping) in the 1940s that is now known simply by his name, J. B. Hunt.[27] Hauling farm products and supplies rather than manufactured goods, Estes, Hunt, and others like them were the young drivers usually found behind the wheels of the earliest "big rigs," the diesel powered trucks that came to prominence in the late '20s.[28] With engines often beneath their cabs (called cab-overs), such things as visibility and turning radius gradually improved, especially as city delivery increased. Soon enough, sleeping compartments, hydraulic brakes, and other improvements were added, and in one year alone Mack's diesel sales jumped 118 percent.[29]

By 1929, yet another former farm boy, A. J. Harrell, had gone from a horse and mule transport business to what would become another of the nation's biggest trucking firms, Yellow Freight (today YRC), thanks initially to the localized hauling needs of oil and gas companies in Oklahoma. He started with only two four-cylindered, straight-bodied trucks operating between Tulsa and Oklahoma City and, according to the book *Yellow in Motion,* this original investment and smart mergers would lead to 18 Yellow Freight terminals stretching strategically throughout the Midwest by 1952.[30]

Obviously, given the right circumstances, trucking was an easy business to get into. Along with avoiding the painful separation required of down-on-their-luck farmers forced to leave the family homestead for work in the cities, "many found that buying a truck could provide enough income to keep a family afloat." That's how Hamilton phrased the basic motivation that led to sales of 150,000 bought or leased trucks in the 1920s and early '30s. After World War I, the U.S. Department of Agriculture (USDA) sought to get farmers "out of the mud" by improving roads to bring their products to market, but in so doing they also stimulated truck manufacturers to convert urban delivery vehicles to rural road machines and for decades these independent truckers and the companies they spawned would shape a newly constituted transportation industry.[31]

Meanwhile, although initially supportive of the rural truckers who helped bring produce and people to their depots in the early 1900s, the railroads became increasingly suspicious of the competitive threat posed by these new entrepreneurs. In fact, railroad managers worried that trucks would soon take over all short-haul traffic, eliminating many of their most profitable routes and capturing many of their best customers. Over short distances, truckers could easily undercut the railroad rates as well as providing faster, point-to-point service.[32]

In addition, with more and more truckers entering the field, tactics for acquiring new business became more and more intense, chaotic, and cutthroat. That's why the railroads and labor were among those that applauded the most when Congress implemented the Motor Carrier Act of 1935, the federal government's effort to regulate trucking much as it had regulated the railroads[33] - even though (as we shall see) it did not apply to the agricultural trucking that had been at the industry's roots. Suddenly, new trucking firms needed more than just a truck and trailer to open for business; they also needed to gain "operating authority." This could be granted between states by the federal government's governing agency, the Interstate Commerce Commission (ICC), but only after usually lengthy and expensive proceedings.[34] In the same way, public service commissions were put in charge of route authority for individual companies within their own state.[35] These newly certified trucking companies had to publish their routes and rates, which the ICC administered to prevent price-cutting.[36]

Over the next four decades plus, these regulations created significant barriers to the further development of new trucking companies, while the largest firms, already in place, generally benefitted and prospered. These included companies like Yellow Freight, Roadway, and Consolidated Freightways. Although never enjoying a monopoly, the largest companies gradually bought out smaller ones, consolidating their control over key markets by eliminating competition.[37] The American Trucking Association, which had been founded to promote self-regulation, became the leading proponent of the new regulations and the International Brotherhood of Teamsters (IBT) also benefited from the industry's suddenly regulated structure, organizing and converting many drivers to union membership despite initial resistance from the largest trucking firms.[38]

As previously noted, however, even as the Teamsters and large trucking carriers benefited from regulation and its stabilization of wages and profits, the Motor Carrier Act's significant exception was agricultural trucking. Thanks to a clause that became known as the "agricultural exemption," truckers were permitted to haul certain farm products at any rate over any geographical route, an obvious nod to political lobbyists and powerful populist groups (like the National Grange and later Farmers Alliance or Peoples Party) seeking to keep down-on-the-farm trucking independent and unregulated as it had always been.[39]

These advocates apparently struck a congressional chord, emphasizing how trucking regulation would result in serious handicaps for farmers and stockmen by imposing higher and higher rates, the result of what they believed were excessive, built-in profit margins for the railroads. It was a final stab at the railroads, their preconceived supply chain nemesis, and left little doubt how American farmers viewed their past and hoped-for-future when it came to trucking.[40] As multiple Pulitzer historian Doris Kearns Goodwin referenced in her latest award-winner, *The Bully Pulpit,* the ICC's creation in 1887 "to ensure railroad rates were 'reasonable and just'" had never seriously deterred the railroad barons ability to challenge ICC rulings in the courts because they never authorized "specific rates." It was a loophole that helped the railroads cater to their "favored big shippers" while maintaining the necessary public illusion of government supervision.[41] The farmers had long recognized this illusion and were dedicated in their commitment to trucking as a result – further confirmation of the very necessary connection rural America had with early motor freight.

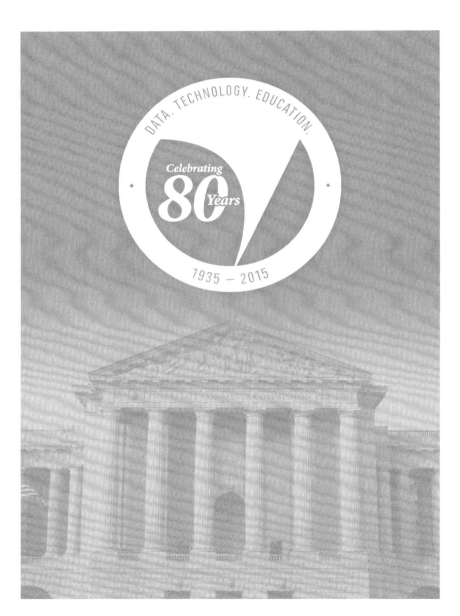

Chapter three
Regulation and Collective Ratemaking

"Shouldn't truckers, the railroads argued before Congress, be regulated by interstate commerce laws just as they were? As it was, truckers enjoyed an unfair advantage." So stated Tom Lewis in his 2013 book *Divided Highways* and as we have seen, the Motor Carriers Act (MCA) of 1935 was largely the result.[42] This acrimony between transportation providers, old and new, and the legislation it prompted, however, wasn't the only major trucking development of the 1930s.

Empowered by the MCA, especially after President Franklin Delano Roosevelt's most controversial depression era agency, the 1933 National Recovery Administration (NRA), was ruled unconstitutional,[43] the ICC was witnessing (and seemingly helpless to stop) the gradual "withering" of railroad lines throughout the country. Lewis compared it to "a great and noble but diseased oak tree. The symptoms had manifested itself at the tips of the branches and they were dying back, slowly in some parts, more rapidly in others."[44]

At the same time, the Great Depression had actually spurred highway funding, as other agencies started by FDR such as the Works Progress Administration (WPA), Public Works Administration (PWA), and Reconstruction Finance Administration (RFA) enjoyed much greater acceptance, and the Bureau of Public Roads became a primary recipient of funding from all three as millions of dollars were spent on putting people back to work via road projects throughout the country.[45] In his epilogue for *The New Deal: A Modern History* published in 2011, Michael Hiltzik pointed out that among its multitude of construction projects, one of those agencies alone, the WPA, was responsible for 651,000 miles of highway, 124,000 new bridges, 84,000 miles of drainage pipes (many of which ran beneath those highways) and 69,000 highway light standards.[46]

Meanwhile, one main provision of the MCA was the requirement that carriers (the still in-vogue term for trucking companies today) were required to make their tariff - defined as "a rate of duty imposed as part of a schedule" - available to the shipping public.[47] This proved an onerous task for the fledgling carriers, who were much more interested in spending their time getting freight on and off their trucks, and promoted the banding together of companies regionally, where they could share resources and develop common and consistent rates for general commodities. According to *Encouraging Cooperation Among Competitors,* published in 1987, this type of collective ratemaking was an arrangement "whereby groups of motor carriers (could) discuss, agree on, and then publish collective tariffs, which establish(ed) the price and terms for motor carrier service under antitrust immunity granted by the Reed-Bulwinkle Act."[48] Ironically, Reed-Bulwinkle didn't come along until 1948 and despite Harry Truman's presidential veto; at least a dozen years after this banding had already begun with governmental acknowledgement and acceptance.[49] Although hinting at possible collusion, that perceived threat was much later in coming.

A 1983 report to the President and Congress by a Motor Carrier Ratemaking Study Commission defined rate bureaus as "organized along geographic and commodity lines" to provide "the administrative machinery by which carriers collectively consider, debate, decide, and publish rates pertaining to the traffic they handle as well as a variety of support services." It also concluded the ratemaking process tended to be dominated by the larger carriers.[50]

Nevertheless, by the late '30s, nonprofit associations had sprouted all across the country with the ICC's blessing for the expressed purpose of establishing and making their regionally agreed-upon rates available to the public. After all, with operating authorities governing (and determining) routes, the still immature trucking industry was regionalized with few truckers traveling very far from home.[51] Among the original rate bureaus that emerged were the New England Motor Rate Bureau, the Connecticut Eastern Motor Freight Rate Conference, the Western Mountain Rate Bureau, the Middle Atlantic Conference, the Niagara Frontier Tariff Bureau, the Eastern Central Association, the Central States Motor Freight Bureau, the Central and Southern Rate Association, the Southwestern Motor Conference, the Middlewest Motor Freight Bureau, the Rocky Mountain Motor Tariff Bureau, the Pacific Inland Tariff Bureau, and, of course, the Southern Motor Carriers Rate Conference.[52] Of those, the Connecticut Eastern, Southwestern, and Western Mountain merged early on with others, leaving ten that would retain collective ratemaking authority for their sections and routes for the next 50-plus years.[53]

Z. L. Pearson of Denver, Colorado was one of the bureau general managers during the majority of those regulation years. As a retired former head of the Rocky Mountain Motor Tariff Bureau, he said, "It all goes back to the railroads and the fact the motor carriers just copied them. The railroads had always had their freight bureaus, so the concept just came from them."

A native of Idaho, where his part-time job while still in high school involved "icing rail cars" for the transport of fresh produce moving east from the West Coast, he joined the Rocky Mountain Bureau 19 years after its founding in 1939. Like the others, it came about largely through the efforts of trucking executives in a particular region banding together to jointly decide and publish rates for the various commodities, all with approval of the ICC. And like so many other trucking firms of the time, many of which became unionized or consumed by larger companies, two that he recalled as founders of the Rocky Mountain association - Milne Truck Lines, Inc., of St. George, Utah and Garrett Freight Lines of Pocatello, Idaho - have long since passed out of business.[54] In 1987, Milne finally fell victim to the Teamster invasion dating from the 1930s and '40s that forced them to pay higher wages than their non-unionized competition. Even earlier (1978), family-owned Garrett Freight Lines had been purchased and absorbed by a larger, more nationally motivated brand, following years spent legally fighting off similar "predators."[55] In fact, of the 100 most prominent early American trucking companies featured in a 2008 book by trucking aficionado Ron Adams called *The Long Haul,* only two exist with their original names today - New Penn and Old Dominion.[56] Like Garrett, many of the others became acquisitions or were consolidated under other names – good examples being Yellow Freight, which was united with Roadway as YRC, and Overnite Transportation, now UPS Freight.[57]

Again, according to Shane Hamilton in *Trucking Country,* "The International Brotherhood of Teamsters (IBT) benefited greatly from the new regulated structure" of the mid 1900s, as the MCA "provided a powerful tool for organizing truck drivers across regions." As a result of the legislation limiting competition in geographic areas, while also requiring all U. S. motor carriers to publish their rates and routes, each regulated trucking firm had further incentive to charge the same rates. If one company felt the need to raise rates to accommodate unionization, other firms had little motivation in those early days to resist. They too could easily raise their own, matching rates. Thus, the 1935 Motor Carrier Act created what has been termed "a free rider effect," permitting the Teamsters to somewhat monopolize the trucking labor market.[58] In the book *Sweatshops on Wheels,* a former truck driver turned researcher and author expressed this trend in a more positive way when he wrote:

> "While regulation did not raise wage rates directly, rate regulation provided the foundation for improving truckers' wages and working conditions and the Teamsters Union became the vehicle for that improvement."[59]

At the same time, consolidation of companies, with its addition by subtraction, took place as a means of accumulating more and more operating authorities (routes) and overcoming unionization. Both were the case for Consolidated Freightways, an early industry giant. According to a corporate history named for its very successful descendent company, *The Legend of Con-way*, Consolidated Freight's 50th anniversary was approaching in the late '70s and its routes covered more than 100,000 miles. It had 267 terminals in 47 states and five Canadian provinces. It had the most complete, single-line service on the largest route system in the United States and Canada, and its Freightliner subsidiary ranked among America's largest 500 industrial corporations based on sales."[60] With all that success, hardly seemed the time to change, right?

Wrong . . . instead, former Con-way President, CEO, and Chairman of the Board Raymond O'Brien admitted as much in his forward to that book. For which he wrote:

"When the trucking industry was regulated, you were able to pass along increases created by inefficiencies to the customer. Then, when deregulation occurred, vast competition arose that wasn't beholden to traditional labor contracts. This created a new environment, where the loyalty of the employees was to the company rather than to a union."[61]

Already, Consolidated Freightways had been busy buying up smaller companies. It had acquired routes all across the country and after forming three entirely "autonomous companies" from those acquisitions, Con-way Central Express, Con-way Western Express, and Con-way Eastern Express (formally Penn-Yan Express), the dominoes were in place for the beginning of the end of Consolidated Freightways and its Teamster commitment. By then merging those three new companies (along with later southern and southwestern acquisitions) without any existing labor contracts and all under the same banner, Con-way Transportation Services was born, union free[62].

But business gambles of that type were few and far between during the years Pearson and his fellow GMs were overseeing the bureaus, printing reams and reams of published tariffs, an essential part of the regulated landscape for carriers and shippers alike. He remembered: "We were there to find out what the (carrier) owners really wanted and needed, and to coordinate efforts for the benefit of the industry by publishing rates in our section of the country. Regular meetings occurred every month and even shippers made rate recommendations on which the carriers would vote up or down. Periodically, carriers would also feel the need to increase all their rates by two to five percent, which had to be filed (and justified) with the ICC and was often protested by shippers. Many times those kinds of increases ended up being litigated before the ICC, similar to the courts."[63]

Due to antitrust laws, the bureaus were not allowed to come together and discuss rates on a collective basis. However, that didn't stop a generation of the general managers from becoming acquainted and meeting informally to share ideas or discuss common concerns. Many, in fact, would remain life-long friends and travel companions.

One of those was the previously mentioned Farriba. In remembering those days, he said, "Most bureaus had a Standing Rate Committee (SRC) of three or four full-time staffers, whose decisions would be published as announcements in their weekly bulletins or as proposals for everyone to consider. The Standing Rate Committee could approve or reject new rates based on the information submitted or pass it on to the General Rate Committee (GRC) for a vote at monthly meetings."

This GRC consisted of carrier members at each bureau who volunteered to serve one-year terms and were re-constituted annually. At the same time, changes approved by the GRC amounted to only a fraction of the overall changes re-published in the bureau tariffs. The far greater percentage of changes to the tariffs came as the result of independent action by individual carriers -- changes that could apply to just one carrier or to more than one if others asked to be included. Shippers were also given the opportunity to support, oppose, or voice their concerns in writing or by making a personal appearance at the GRC meetings.

"All tariff publications contained an issue date and an effective date, and each publication had to be on file in the ICC office in Washington, D.C., for at least 30 days before it could be effective," Farriba continued. "At the same time, the ICC could and did suspend many changes that had previously been protested by an interested party, be they carrier, shipper, or whomever. As a result, at Southern Motor Carriers, we allowed 45 days from the issue date to the effective date, so that everyone had sufficient time for review and the implementation of changes."[64]

Also among that generation of GMs was Jack Fraser at the Boston-based New England Motor Rate Bureau, who like Farriba didn't retire until 1996. Unlike Farriba, however, Fraser was witness to his bureau on its last legs. Of that time he said, "After deregulation, Southern Motor Carriers was the only one to make it big. The rest of us went out gradually. From 110 employees we were down to five or six by the time I retired. Believe me, it was not a pleasant last couple of years having to lay off all those people."[65]

And taking those sentiments a step further, Pearson, whose Rocky Mountain Motor Tariff Bureau went out of business in 2000, said, "Taking over for Vernon, Jack (Middleton) was able to keep together a nucleus of carriers and coordinate with shippers for a corporate structure at Southern Motor Carriers that the rest of us couldn't match. He deserves a lot of credit for that."[66]

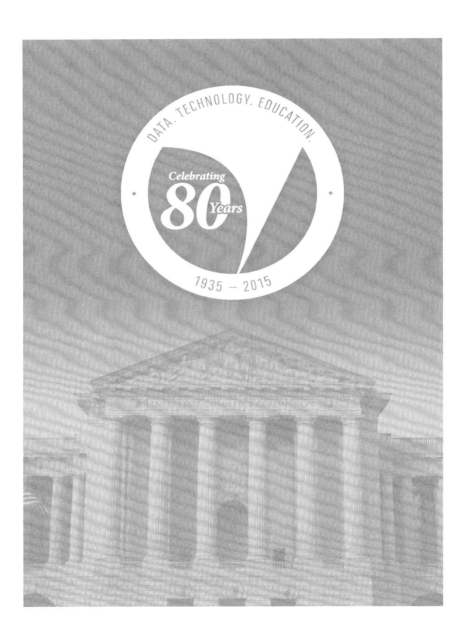

Chapter four
The Interstate Transformation

Amidst this era of rate bureaus, something outside the industry would forever change transportation and the movement of motor freight in the United States. In fact, it would alter and accelerate American life in ways not previously anticipated. While new and improved roadways were already becoming more evident throughout the country as the nation became a population of one and even two-car families, the Interstate Highway System, a dream as far back as FDR's days in the White House, finally became reality under President Dwight Eisenhower. Just as FDR had once drawn six lines across a U.S. map with three running east to west, ocean to ocean, and three others running from Canada to Mexico, all while instructing his Bureau of Public Roads to come up with a plan for modern, multi-lane highways connecting the nation's largest metropolitan areas, coast to coast . . . so, too, FDR's general, the one who had led Allied forces to victory in Europe during the excruciating interlude of World War II and experienced Germany's modern Autobahn highway firsthand, wasn't about to let such a great idea fade away, especially after becoming President.[67]

Even before "I like Ike" became the rallying cry of voters across the nation, trucking had grown enormously. The first registration of trucks in the U.S. in 1904 revealed 700 such vehicles in operation. In 1939, 35 years later, that number had already risen to 4.5 million with an equally significant increase in carrying capacity . . . and that number (and capacity) would more than double by the 1950s.[68]

According to *Divided Highways,* "ample evidence" also existed by the '50s that highway builders and users had joined with automobile makers to actively lobby for more and better roads, as "Americans chose to abandon the antiquated railroads for their over-crowded highways."[69] And the same book confirms that it took from April 1954 to July 1956 for Eisenhower to barter his renewed idea through Congress. Along with a reluctant government, Eisenhower had to battle his way through health issues, including a heart attack that disabled him for six weeks and an operation that weakened him for four more. To pay for his Interstate System, some argued for a national system of toll roads as already existed on turnpikes in Pennsylvania, New Jersey, and Maine, while others felt everything would work better as a 50-50 split between the states and federal government. Regardless, Eisenhower figured it would take $5 billion a year for 10 years and finally, after much compromise and the President's determined urgency, the Federal Highway Act of 1956 passed both houses of Congress . . . and with it the accompanying Highway Revenue Act - to pay for it all.[70]

Thirty-five years later (or a quarter of a century longer than originally thought), the original plan was finally finished at a total cost of $425 billion and America had become totally dependent on trucks.[71] In fact, shipping by trucks increased 257 percent between 1955 and 1990 as the Interstate Highways created what *Divided Highways* called "commercial channels for the shipping of goods" just as mighty rivers, man-made canals, and the Great Lakes had served in that capacity during the country's earliest years.[72] From the Interstate Highways and the 1960s on, bigger and bigger trucks carried the load and the fact this rise in motor freight followed construction of our modern highway system came as "no great surprise."

Indeed, even before the '60s passed, the dominating influence of trucks on our first interstates was being felt. Instead of being housed in multi-storied buildings near city centers, industries were already moving away from crowded downtowns to suburbs and near the new or soon to be finished interstates. By the late 1970s, it had become possible to ship goods several hundred miles overnight by truck. And again, according to, *Divided Highways,* that's what paved the way to yet another important trucking change – when American industries began adopting a sophisticated system originally developed in Japan and known as Just-In-Time Production. Utilizing this approach, industries no longer had to store large quantities of parts. Instead, they relied on trucks loaded with new supplies arriving continuously in a system that was both complex and fragile, but also one that proved remarkably efficient, especially given the new and constantly improving support of such things as computer software and global tracking systems.[73]

"Manufacturers (had) turned the highway system into a vast rolling and fluid warehouse" despite threats either labor-related or catastrophic weather-induced. You might even say the revamped American supply chain was born on these interconnected ribbons of concrete that entered (and exited) the public domain amidst a baby-boomer generation learning to navigate a nation of freeways. Suddenly, 18-wheelers were everywhere and going in every direction.

Fifty percent of all truck traffic was already on the young and still multiplying interstates by the year 1970, even as infrastructure stresses - such as already crumbling new highways under the increased capacities of heavier trucks - began to occur. Initial lessons had to be learned and construction adjustments made to accommodate this modern mode of commerce,[74] a factor made increasingly obvious by the proliferation of the individual states' interstate highway weigh stations ever since.

At the same time, new terminology entered the motor freight lexicon to help distinguish the type of hauls carriers were being asked to make. As defined by that same former truck driver turned research scientist, Michael Belzer, these included: interline - "a single freight movement shared by at least two carriers, neither of which can deliver the freight within its own system," and front haul - "the primary freight loading from a trucker's home terminal to the consignee." Another was line-haul, intended simply as "an over-the-road freight movement."[75]

Perhaps the most important new terms from business or historical perspectives, however, were truckload (TL) and less-than-truckload (LTL). The first was defined as "a shipment weighing more than 10,000 pounds," but it was also used to identify "the type of carrier primarily hauling large shipments," operations not requiring a terminal. The second would develop to mean "a shipment weighing fewer than 10,000 pounds," but also to help identify "carriers who primarily haul smaller shipments." A full trailer for an LTL carrier typically consists of 20 or 30 separate shipments and usually requires elaborate terminal, pickup, and/or delivery procedures.[76]

These would come into play more and more after deregulation in 1980. Early in *Sweatshops on Wheels,* Belzer set the stage for this evolving difference when he wrote:

"Competition would come to divide general commodity trucking into two segments, less-than-truckload (LTL) and truckload (TL). Less-than-truckload carriers maintained and even extended their terminal network, which was needed to sort and re-ship their small cargo (averaging perhaps 1,200 pounds). Truckload carriers got rid of (their) existing terminal structure and focused on large shipments that they picked up from a shipper and delivered directly to consignees."[77]

There were even significant contrasts among major companies handling both LTL and TL shipments.

In *Yellow In Motion,* James Filgas and L. L. Waters briefly compared Yellow Freight and Roadway. Ironically now combined as YRC (as previously noted), they made the point that while Yellow "seemed to expand extensively rather than intensively" with rather long average line-haul and a high percentage of business that was truckload by 1972, Roadway always "restricted its early activities to intensive development east of the Mississippi." That variance in strategies posed greater adjustment problems for Yellow Freight once deregulation came along in the 1980s.[78]

Such future differences in motor freight were hardly on President Eisenhower's mind, however, when he followed the path of former transportation trendsetters by taking his Interstate Highway System from concept to legislative conquest and confirmation in 1956. In so doing, he not only imitated George Washington's career as general turned President, but also his foresight in locating the nation's capital city on the transportation conducive Potomac River with direct access to both the new nation's interior and the Chesapeake Bay, as well as later transportation giants like DeWitt Clinton (Erie Canal) and Abraham Lincoln (transcontinental railroad) – leaders who understood where the future was headed and how best to facilitate getting us there.[79]

Unfortunately, the same could probably not be said for most Presidents or Congresses when it came to the rate bureaus. According to a book edited by Grant M. Davis in 1980, *Collective Ratemaking in the Motor Carrier Industry,* the purpose of rate bureaus was more often than not misunderstood in the halls of Washington, D.C. Frequently portrayed as "cartels," by elected officials, the "orderly functions" they brought to the industry would eventually be extinguished in a rush to marketplace judgement. For almost five decades, however, their very tedious system and services were a mainstay and foundation for American business.[80] In that regard, their intricate structure and painstaking processes are well worth remembering.

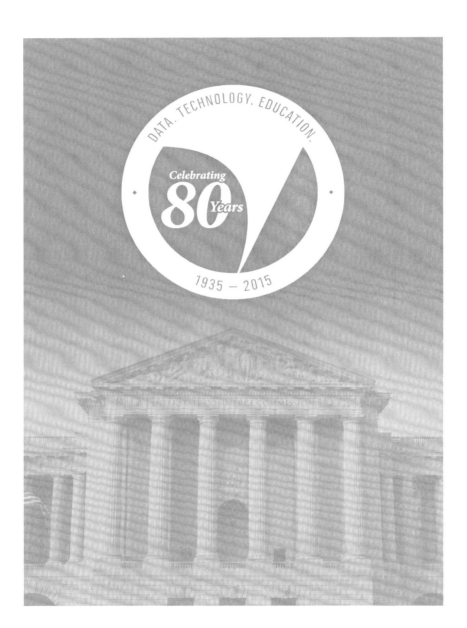

Chapter five
Looking Back at Bureau Days

Perhaps no one better exemplifies the first 50-plus years that Southern Motor Carriers spent as a bureau for the motor freight industry than Leajar Brooks. From mail clerk to offset pressman; from tariff compiler to freight auditor; from manager of the Rate and Research Departments to, you name it and Brooks just about did it all.

Growing up in Buford, Georgia, eventually one of Atlanta's far-flung suburbs but in those days a separate town about 35 miles away, Brooks was like many mid teens by the time he was in high school, anxious to make some money. His first part-time job was at a local gas station and by the time his last high school summer vacation rolled around and his hours stretched to full time, the station owner felt sufficiently confident in the 17-year-old's dependability and integrity to entrust him with running the place for three days, just long enough for him to visit his brother in Florida. So, entrusting him with a cigar box to keep proceeds in while he was away, the owner's brotherly visit was made, much to the chagrin of friends and townspeople who couldn't believe he was leaving such a responsibility to someone so young. Little did Brooks know the planned excursion was also a test.

A test that he would pass with flying colors, because upon the owner's return, he found out that with everything in perfect order, his boss actually had in mind another nearby station he was hoping to purchase with the intention of putting his young (and now proven) protégé in charge once he graduated from high school. It was an early indication of the confidence and work ethic Brooks would inspire throughout his life, and especially his 43 years at SMC.

Instead, following work as a saddle maker at a local company for two years after high school (including a special one for early Western movie star Lash LaRue), Brooks' girlfriend questioned the future of saddle making as a career, prompting her future husband to seek a different job in the nearby big city, where she was already employed. That's how, armed with two want ads from two Spring Street establishments in Atlanta, Brooks made the bus trip from Buford in early January 1952 and interviewed for clerk positions at both Southern Motor Carriers and a nearby auto parts store. Two days later, when both called to offer their vacant positions, his choice of the bustling SMC Mailroom proved the first step in a career path that would make him fairly typical of the organization's pioneers.

"I liked being busy and SMC was a busy place," Brooks recalled. "Not many people ever knew what a rate bureau did and I sure didn't before I applied, but I could tell that it was a place full of hard working people and that appealed to me. Starting out in the Mailroom, I felt I had a future in a place with advancement opportunities."[81]

And as already established, advance he did, all the way to the senior management level. In fact, it was Brooks who would ensure the organization's success and outreach long after its bureau days were over by his decision to hire the young and aspiring Middleton while he was still a student at Georgia State University. "Evelyn Sutton, the lady who handled human resources, knew I needed a rate clerk, and she called me and said she had a young man she wanted me to interview. So Jack came in and impressed me with how sincere he was and how much he needed a position to help with his college expenses. I think I hired him on the spot, but a day later, he got another job offer from a place he had also applied, Brown Transport, and he came to me and said 'Mr. Brooks, I have this other offer that will pay more, but I like it here and need to see if you could give me a raise to their level. When I told him that was impossible right then, he felt compelled to type up a nice resignation letter even though he had only been there such a short time and left to take the job with Brown. However, a day or two later he was back, telling me he liked our job much better than theirs and hoping our job was still available, even at the lower pay. Well, I was happy to tell him it was and the rest is history, although he hadn't been there long when Lester Mann (CFO), who was over SMC Accounting for years, came to me and said, 'Leajar, I want Middleton for my department.' His major at Georgia State was accounting, so that made sense even though I knew I would be losing a very promising rate clerk."[82]

In fact, as a result of Brooks working alongside Farriba for so many years and then being responsible for Middleton's arrival, it's probably safe to say that Brooks, as much as anyone, bridged the passing of the SMC leadership baton. That's why his knowledge of those bureau years remains so creditable and important to this story.

Through Brooks' eyes one can glimpse the original SMC property at 873 Spring Street as well as the eventual move to more spacious (and prestigious) 1307 Peachtree, across the street from Atlanta's High Museum of Art. Through his knowledge, one gains an understanding of the inner-workings of the rate bureau before deregulation.

Both locations featured multiple levels and no less than eight on-site departments, as well as one with representatives dispersed throughout the Southeast. An average of 150 SMC staffers was necessary for the very hands-on activity that took place each and every weekday for the benefit of motor carriers and shippers throughout the region.

Into this world of constant change and publication, the Mailroom Department that Brooks first encountered would have contained approximately ten people primarily employed to produce and distribute the *Southern Motor Carrier Docket Bulletin,* which went out to three or four hundred carrier members as well as two to three thousand shippers weekly. Filled with pending rate proposals requested by individual carriers in one of nine southeastern states, these had to first be scrutinized by the Standing Rate Committee (SRC), which was made up of four men, all SMC employees who evaluated those proposals as they came in, received feedback on each one via the *Bulletin,* and two weeks later would "review, comment, adopt, change, or delete" the recommended rate changes. They might also pass them on to the monthly General Rate Committee Meetings, which were mostly held in Atlanta and open (for voting purposes) to all southeastern carrier members.[83]

Pros and cons of the newly proposed rates could be debated by carriers and shippers alike through correspondence, or in person at the GRC meetings with evidence both for and against being given consideration before a vote was taken. One of the most remembered of those meetings occurred in the late 1970s, when multi-pickup discounts being offered by some of the larger LTL carriers were scheduled for discussion. That was something sure to negatively impact many of the smaller carriers of the region. This was apparently especially so in and around Nashville, Tennessee, where a sizable contingent of concerned Volunteer Staters decided to charter a plane to Atlanta the day of the GRC and then bus from the airport to the meeting for a more sizable in-room presence whenever the multi-pickup discounts came up. Their mass entrance that day would go down in trucker and bureau lore as arrival of the "Tennessee mafia" and thankfully, when a back room (or bathroom) deal was struck averting the multi-discount considerations,[84] their point had been made and accepted in a very convincing way without (what can now, so many years later, be joked about) any bloodshed.

Needless to say, SMC's *Docket Bulletin* made for essential reading for any carrier and quite often shippers whenever it arrived in the mail each week. Livelihoods were at stake and a say in the collective process had to always be on the minds of people who moved freight in the South - as it's certain they were with the arrival of similar weekly bulletins from other bureaus throughout the nation.

While the *Bulletin* and smaller supplements were printed on an off-set press located in the Mailroom at SMC, the much larger tariff books, which were updated with the most current rate changes about every three weeks, were handled by a nearby professional printer, Stein Printing Company. These books were also critical to all shipping and carrier business, functioning as the local industry bible on a daily basis until the very next addition (bought and paid for each time) came along.

Preparing these tomes of commodity specific rates was the job of the Rate Department, approximately 40 staffers strong and divided equally into sections with names like South-East, South-Southwest, and for a time, because there were so many textile mills in the southern United States, one referred to simply as Textile. These small, sub-groups of about seven staffers each were charged with checking all past and present rates as well as current rail routes, a necessary component when it came to getting each *Bulletin* ready for press. In addition, all in-bound mail had to come through the Rate Department and large bags full of correspondence would daily be filtered by the general rate clerk, who sorted and assessed to whom each piece would be routed.

Likewise, the Tariff Department averaged more than 50 staffers with lots of turnover. It was responsible for the very tedious process of continuously preparing and updating approximately 75 tariff books, ranging from 40 to 500 pages each, by hand. That's right, according to Brooks, this was done longhand and by manually pasting the new rates into the previous books using rubber cement, an early form of cut-and-paste, if you will, before computers. Supplements would also be issued on a two to three-week cycle, depending on the rate and rate activity, but the ICC controlled the number of supplements that could be available at any one time.[85]

For many years, Dean Stowers was chief of tariff with his name proudly displayed on the front of every tariff book published. "We were the revenue producing department," he emphasized. "We were responsible for sales of the tariffs (the books) and for getting new customers, which I did many times. I still want credit for Old Dominion Freight and Averitt Express, two of the biggest freight lines in the South. They came on board during my tenure and through my efforts and they've been with us ever since."[86]

There was also a minimal Legal Department of three to four people, including at least two practitioners. These practitioners did not have to be practicing attorneys, but they did have to at least be qualified to practice before the ICC. Regular legal representation was also maintained in Washington, D.C., as well as Atlanta.

Meanwhile, the Cost Department consisted of seven to ten number crunchers. To them, carrier members sent copies of freight bills as well as monthly and yearly reports, so that all might be combined, averaged, and analyzed in putting the best foot forward from a regional standpoint anytime a case needed to be made for wholesale rate increases with the ICC. Economics differed greatly from region to region, so substantial evidence had to be maintained and presented whenever membership prerogatives needed to be expressed at the national level and these SMC staffers were the ones charged with keeping such evidence relevant.

Added to these in-house departments was an in-house Maintenance staff; Accounting, where all payroll and human resource functions were handled and where, as already mentioned, Middleton's extraordinary rise really started; and the Administration, which consisted of the executive VP and general manager, their highly-efficient administrative secretaries, and occasionally an assistant GM. There were usually at least eight people in Accounting and no less than three in Maintenance.

At the same time, one early, off-site department was Weighing and Research (later shortened to just Research and recalled to Atlanta), which consisted of four individual representatives strategically located throughout the Southeast who represented carrier members with shippers whenever weight or packaging problems arose. This service eliminated the necessity for carriers to deal with such issues themselves, an obvious time and public relations benefit provided by the bureau.[87]

Looking Back at Bureau Days 33

As already indicated, early SMC presidents were actually the head of the Board of Governors. The director of the bureau was titled executive vice-president and the second and sometimes third in command, the general manager and assistant GM. Thus Brooks was initially hired by then SMC Assistant General Manager John Shumate. Also, as previously mentioned, SMC's first Executive VP was W. M. Miller, a "very organized and strict" administrator who had gotten his start with the railroads and had railroad bureau experience when he assumed leadership of the organization from an original, three-man Board supervising committee in the late '30s. As Farriba emphasized, "Where else were the early motor freight rate bureau leaders to come from? In those days, no place but the railroad bureaus provided that kind of experience."

Miller was in charge from 1938 through 1964. He was replaced by the previously mentioned Bill Brown, another, who like Farriba, Brooks, and eventually Middleton, rose through the organizational ranks. After heading the Tariff Department before becoming general manager, Brown assumed the executive VP role upon Miller's retirement.[88]

The annual mid-summer General Rate Committee meetings lasted two to three days. They were held at special southeastern resort locations like Savannah, Georgia; Daytona Beach, Florida; and Gatlinburg, Tennessee - for the enjoyment of the gathered membership and their families along with the ongoing business of rates and other bureau issues. By contrast, the monthly rate meetings were held in Atlanta at hotels or other known buildings of the day. Once sufficient debate had been entertained at meetings on requested changes, all shippers in attendance would exit the room during voting, which was for carriers only.

As previously established and indicated by the original promotional map (see photo section), the SMCRC states included Virginia, Kentucky, Tennessee, North Carolina, South Carolina, Mississippi, Alabama, Georgia, and Florida. It was a group with very similar constituencies and interests and a group that included some of the most influential LTL carriers in the country, a group that would largely stay intact and pave the way for SMC to eventually become truly national in scope and service as SMC^3.[89]

Chapter six
Of Zip Codes and Benchmarks

Like so many other young men of the mid to late 1900s, Danny Slaton began a career in transportation as a member of the Teamsters, a union man, whose card-carrying status entitled him to a lot more per hour with Yellow Freight than he would have received doing the same job for smaller, non-unionized carriers. For that reason alone, the Yellow loading docks in Indianapolis was what he termed, "a great college job" while working towards a degree at Indiana University. From there he would go on to various jobs in LTL trucking, including sales and terminal management, before landing a creative assignment as special projects manager for one of the ten remaining motor freight rate bureaus in 1983.[90]

Gas shortages, the Iranian hostage crisis, and the U. S. hockey team's "Miracle on Ice," weren't the only things making news near the end of Jimmy Carter's one term in the White House. Also, somewhat hidden among the major headlines, was the Motor Carrier Act of 1980, designed to reverse its legislative namesake of 1935, when the trucking industry had first been regulated – much, as we've established, the railroads had always been.[91] In his book, *Family Driven,* then Benton Express CEO Herb Matthews pointed out that Carter confidant Bert Lance had assured the American Trucking Association that if elected president in 1976, the ex-Georgia governor "had no intention of deregulating the trucking industry" and "would preserve the integrity of the ICC," but four years later, he did it anyway.[92]

At the time, the "national newspaper of the trucking

industry," *Transport Topics'* announcement of the new MCA enthusiastically stated, "The bill would relax entry requirements, ease operating restrictions, introduce more pricing freedom, and phase out single-line collective ratemaking."[93] On the other hand, the rate bureaus were officially on notice. Although they had seen it coming for a number of years, confidence was shaken. They now had to come up with new ideas and new roles to ensure their relevance in what seemed destined to be a very different and deregulated transportation landscape from the one they had been born into in the mid 1930s.

Slaton was one of a new breed being looked to in making that transition. When he was hired by the Louisville, Kentucky-based Central and Southern bureau in 1983, it was with the understanding that he would help develop marketing for new products that would soon be in demand in a rapidly changing, deregulated marketplace.[94]

Officially named the Central and Southern Motor Tariff Association (CSA), it came to be known as "an overhead bureau," according to its last general manager, John Womack, meaning a bureau without one clearly defined territory, but instead, one that crossed over to handle routes between two territories; in this case the Southeast and the north central states of Ohio, Michigan, Indiana, and Illinois.[95] As a rule, this split designation actually resulted in a much smaller carrier membership than other bureaus that represented and serviced one specific region of the country.

Nevertheless, while not having "a home constituency," a perceived weakness that contributed to "something of a complex" among its staff, CSA was not without strengths and under Womack, those same CSA employees "were hungry" in their pursuit of new ideas and investment. This was especially true when it came to the suddenly-exploding world of computerization.

After all, the computer age was dawning and CSA had already become one of the first bureaus with access to a mainframe. And under the leadership of technology whiz Charlie Owen, CSA had, by the time Slaton came on board, begun development of a computer infrastructure and system it planned to share with two other bureaus.[96]

    Owen, a resident of nearby Elizabethton, Kentucky and an early computer systems programmer, had been hired specifically by CSA to make this partnership, with the Central States Bureau (CSB) in Chicago and to a later and lesser degree with the Niagara Frontier Bureau (NFB) in Buffalo, New York, work. Of his first day on the job, he remembered being asked to bring a suitcase for a four-day trip to Chicago, where he and his boss, CSA Technology Manager Rafael Blanco, met with the management at Central States about a massive technology investment CSB had already made. "I was green as a gourd and I wasn't briefed until I got on the airplane," Owen recalled. "The gist of it was that Central States had already spent thousands with IBM in an attempt to begin compiling and publishing computerized tariffs. They had a big mainframe, but they didn't know how to use it. They had no computer people and IBM was trying to get them to spend more to let them develop a program that they would train on before running it themselves. After six months of gathering and analyzing data and another seven or eight going through IBM programs with the idea of being able to run everything on one machine, I was able to recommend existing software for a joint operation between CSA and CSB, with NFB to be added after everything was up and running."[97]

    At that time in the early 1970s, Continuous Traffic Studies (CTS) were documents prepared by each bureau to provide evidence and satisfy the ICC whenever across-the-board rate increases were requested. They also promised to become what Owen termed, "computer resource hogs." However, Dr. Edwards Deeming, a mathematician and engineer of already considerable fame, developed a traffic study whereby samplings of carrier freight bills could be utilized to prove actual average expenses and, taking advantage of this new development, promised the "quicker and cheaper" CTS that every bureau craved. Utilizing remote work stations and telephone lines to connect the mainframe with the partnering bureaus, and converting programs to "a native language" and automatic coding quickly became Owen's priority. Initially this was done on a rudimentary cartho-ray tube, what they called "the big green screen" and eventually the entire CSA Tariff Department, working dual shifts and four-day work weeks, was brought on board to assist with inputting duties.[98]

Julie Beach, a recently retired (2014) SMC[3] vice president and Louisville native, was one of several young CSA programmers who assisted Owen at that time even though hired as a field engineer. She remembered those early days when she remarked, "We were basically developing an electronic data interchange (EDI) and our workload was greatly reduced when we got the Tariff Department involved. They no longer had to just sit there and wait on us to catch up. Shippers were asking that everything be computerized and we were trying to get there by identifying and formatting key elements of data so that it could be transferred over phone lines."[99]

Owen described the resulting momentum at CSA as "impetus" and "industry standard." He also acknowledged how growth of the computer operations naturally followed, resulting in the purchase of the second largest mainframe in all of Louisville at that time. Soon, as many as 15 people were employed in CSA's Computer Services Department.[100]

As a result, this developing computer expertise had the potential to become a new source of income for the smaller and somewhat cash-strapped bureau facing the same deregulation transition (and tension) as all the others. "There's no doubt we became more entrepreneurial and innovative in our approach than the other bureaus," Slaton confirmed. "I was initially hired to develop routing guides (another type of industry publication) and to take better advantage of our large printing operation, which was already taking outside customers, but very quickly that evolved into leveraging our Computer Services, marketing our expertise to individual carriers and other bureaus. With no home court, so to speak, and with deregulation about to take hold, we had to look to new markets if we wanted to stay in business."[101]

In fact, with the advent of microcomputers during the early 1980s, 500-page tariff books, which only large mainframes could previously produce, rate computation became possible at the personal computer (PC) or desktop level. As Slaton added, "The future was obviously the PC in the rate business just like everything else and with some really good technology thinkers, CSA went about developing a bridge to restructure the way rates were provided. I will never forget the day we were in a meeting when Charlie (Owen) broke in to say he had located two PCs in a new computer store on Shelbyville Road that he could buy for about $6,000 each and very quickly Womack said, 'go get 'em.' Everybody knew we had to get our hands on at least one."[102]

CSA saw it coming and was on the leading edge. According to Slaton, it became the Louisville firm's focus and their first product was CZAR, which stood for complete, zip, audit, rating, with the key component being zip codes. It became one of the earliest examples of zip codes dramatically aiding an individual American industry. Rather than having designated routes based on point names, as had always been done by bureaus in the past, the five digit zip codes promised to eliminate overlapping errors and make the process much more efficient and easier to compute.[103]

"We began working with data from all the bureaus and developed CZAR on the mainframe. Actually, I took home the class rates and worked with them for about two weeks on an old TRS-80. That was before IBM unveiled its PCs in 1982," Owen remembered.[104]

At the same time in the midst of deregulation, the industry was becoming much more competitive and attempting to convert to individual company tariffs, especially the largest carriers. "For them it became almost a vanity thing to publish their own tariffs, but only the really big ones had the resources to do it," Slaton emphasized.[105]

To avert this suddenly growing trend, CSA moved ahead with an elaborate deconstructive process. It took months and months of tedious hours, but when complete, it had combined the various bureau matrixes and eliminated all geographic ambiguity; the rating was much faster; and the ability to distribute rates, even before the internet, was much more portable via five-and-a-quarter-inch floppy disks. The new system, which was first labeled CZAR-Lite (keeping original caps and hyphenated) overrode most of the previous point names and set comparable rates based on primary zip codes. Whereas CZAR had required 16 disks for distribution purposes, the new system required only two just a year later. Beach said, "I'll always remember, Keith Brookshire, who was in charge of PC development, said, 'We've got to call this something. Since the first one was CZAR, why not CZAR-Lite?'"[106]

Meanwhile, although sensing CzarLite's potential, the CSA staff had also come to the realization that while equipping the individual carriers by selling their new computerized tool would provide an immediate financial windfall, it could also put them out of business. Instead, due to the innovative thinking of a Detroit-based procurement specialist at Masco Industries, Bill Ball, another approach emerged.

Ball, who Slaton termed an early "thought leader" using today's more modern lexicon, was frustrated by individual carrier tariffs and thought there had to be a way to simplify the shipping process. In fact, he advocated taking Masco's entire supply chain out from under their Traffic Division and moving it under his own management as vice-president for procurement. "He wanted a standard benchmark," Slaton remembered, "so he could go to each of Masco's providers on the carrier side and determine what discounts he could get based on that benchmark." The result: Masco became the first shipper CzarLite was "licensed to."

Indeed, licensing was the key. "Ball became our first commercial customer and the first real proponent of what we were doing with CzarLite," Slaton said. "He was our pioneer - someone who had the foresight and willpower to let carriers know that if they wanted his business they would have to get on board with this new system. In doing so, he also broke the traditional shipper-carrier mold by making it a procurement process."[107]

No doubt, CSA had created a disruption in the computer world – a game-changer. Slaton's original CSA marketing collateral offered CzarLite on a one-time trial basis of just $99 or at an annual entry rate of $799, knowing that anyone who paid for the one-time trial would most likely be back for the annual package in short order. It confidently stated:

> "CzarLite was designed to be the first truly affordable national rating system suitable for mass distribution. This database includes 16 tariffs from the 10 major motor carrier tariff bureaus."[108]

And still exhibiting what must have been their initial sense of accomplishment, the kind experienced when any original concept or time-consuming strategy proves worthy of the effort, Slaton confirmed, "Our first mailing went out to about 60,000 and resulted in stacks and stacks of return postcards for weeks. Pretty soon we realized we had struck a vein of gold."

In no time, CzarLite software users went from zero to several hundred. "We could provide any service where LTL benchmarks could be applied, whatever the individual customer wanted," Slaton continued. "Throughout 1987, we witnessed a rapid ramp-up and saturation of our customer base." Shippers, especially, benefited by the innovation.[109]

At the same time, some of the largest carriers, the ones, as previously noted who had started to publish their own rates as deregulation took hold, were not initially happy about CzarLite, especially as more and more shippers demanded its use from a benchmark/consistency standpoint. For several years thereafter, their grumblings had to be dealt with at both GRC meetings and Board meetings, according to Middleton.[110]

Meanwhile, other competitive products were developed by outside consultants. But whereas these cost hundreds of thousands of dollars, the CSA introductory price of less than $800 was obviously special and with bureau rates constantly changing, CzarLite also offered regular updates over the renewable 12-month period thanks, once again, to the established benchmarks. In fact, as development continued, there was a huge challenge to keep up with available data and to understand the intricacies of all LTL ratings. That was the critical path most outside developers were not willing to take.

Soon enough, the next step had to be some sort of application program interface (API), which required software pros to build a PC-based rating engine in the hope that the re-keying of all shipment data could be bypassed. In other words, in order to produce computerized rates on a stand-alone personal computer, each carrier's shipment profiles needed to be inputted electronically from another, previous source. "We had to have a sort of black box rating engine," Slaton stated. "We needed a way for machines to talk to each other and to accomplish that we had to give outside technology pros access to our (so-called) black box."

From this final step, CSA became the first bureau to use benchmarking in the development of a Windows-based rating system. "It was all very entrepreneurial on our part," Slaton said. "We were innovating to fit the needs of a deregulated marketplace and creating a disruption in that marketplace at the same time."

Competition, even among the individual bureaus, was rising. Outsiders were getting involved with different opportunities and new ideas. In particular, because of CSA's and SMC's overlapping territory and memberships, carriers in the Southeast were questioning why both were needed. Or, at the very least, why the two bureaus weren't cooperating? "We were both doing many of the same things for the same carriers, which didn't make sense," Slaton acknowledged.[111]

Into this thought process the word "merger" first appeared and the Boards of both SMC and CSA began to actively discuss the idea. The real question was which bureau would have the surviving identity?[112] Regardless, the futures of Owen, Beach, and Slaton would remain tied to the technology they first developed and made known to the industry in 1987, something they would continue to do for the surviving identity in the years ahead.

Chapter seven
Surviving Identity

An attorney by trade, a respected veteran of the railroads that gave him his start, and a somewhat self-proclaimed transportation expert, Womack ran the Central and Southern Motor Freight Tariff Association (CSA) from 1965 to 1988.[113] Aggressive as a rule, as evidenced by CSA's early technology efforts, he nevertheless may have been at his most aggressive behind the scenes in his desire to see his Central and Southern bureau consume the one in Atlanta, especially once merger discussions for the two became commonplace in the 1970s.[114]

At the same time, J. Harwood Cochrane was the esteemed leader of Overnite Transportation in Richmond, Virginia, the company that for $1.25 billion in cash in May 2005 would become UPS Freight, the LTL branch of global giant United Parcel Service (UPS). Cochrane, who would live into his 100s, started his career in trucking as so many other young southerners, hauling produce,[115] and by the time the mid-1970s rolled around, he was serving as president of the Southern Motor Carriers Rate Conference (SMCRC or just SMC). In fact, he was president at the time of a January 29, 1975, meeting in Atlanta when the Boards of CSA and SMC got together and officially broached the subject of merger for the first time.[116]

According to Womack's eventual counterpart at SMC, Vernon Farriba, talk of merging the two bureaus had actually started as far back as the early '70s, when several leading carrier companies had representatives on both Boards. Ryder Truck Lines out of Jacksonville, Florida was one of those. The president of the CSA Board was the president of Ryder at the same time SMC had a Ryder vice-president serving on its Board . . . and Ryder wasn't the only carrier with such proximity to both. Obviously, that was a situation that encouraged shared knowledge. In other words, it was a built-in recipe for turmoil or, if nothing else, conflict of interest between the bureaus.

"It was on the minds of the southern carriers because many had leadership on both Boards," Farriba said. "They were paying for tariff books, dues, and other expenses from both bureaus and had begun asking the question 'why should we have to keep dealing with both of you,' with their next response almost always being, 'you should merge.'"[117]

At the time, SMC probably had three times as many members as CSA with better management and more financial stability. As established, CSA, which (remember) only served between the South and central states in the North, was developing the better technology.[118]

Such was the situation when that 1975 meeting was jolted by a surprise resolution. To this day, Farriba believes it was engineered by Womack and part of "some back stage politicking" when it came to his desire to see SMC taken over by CSA. But far more surprising is the fact the resolution that day was entered by Cochrane - the Southern Motor Carriers president.[119]

While neither Womack nor his Atlanta counterpart at the time, Bill Brown, was in attendance at the Boards-only meeting, the resolution did read like a spur-of-the-moment, handwritten takeover bid. Taken point-by-point it resolved:

"1. That John Womack be charged with the total management of both CSA and SMCRC.

2. That CSA and SMCRC elect a Special Executive Committee comprised of three directors from each Board and that this Special Executive Committee elect its own chairman.

3. That John Womack be responsible in his dual management role to the Special Executive Committee.

4. That the Special Executive Committee members be responsible to their respective bureau Boards.

5. That Womack be instructed to work with the Special Executive Committee towards the implementation of the cost-reducing consolidation as outlined in (a previous) study.

6. That Womack and the Special Executive Committee would be further charged with the possibility of making recommendations toward the possible merger of the two bureaus, including a recommendation as to the appropriate location of the merged facilities.

7. That both the CSA and SMCRC Boards fully and enthusiastically support Womack in this management role.

8. Approval of this Resolution is subject to the affirmative opinion of counsel of each bureau."[120]

Quick and disturbingly easy, it probably would have resolved the merger issue right then and there if not for the last stipulation (No. 8). After all, it did receive an affirmative vote from the gathered Boards and Southern Motor Carriers was on the verge of extinction before its leadership even knew what had happened.[121] "There's no doubt in my mind they would have just closed us if CSA had been placed in charge," Middleton has often maintained in the years since.[122]

Luckily for the Atlanta-based bureau, however, the lawyers' opinions did matter and as soon as the SMC legal team got wind of what was in the works, they produced irrefutable reasons as to why this action couldn't go down that way. Instead, it was agreed during further meetings the next day that the leadership of both bureaus would develop simultaneous merger plans that should be examined and discussed before either plan or combination of plans was adopted in the future.[123]

That's how close present day SMC[3] came to being CSA. At the same time, the question must be asked why the SMC president would have offered such a surprising resolution, unless in league with Womack, especially given the loyalty typically evidenced by the SMC Board. Perhaps the answer can be found in SMC's change of leadership a year later, when Brown was relieved of his duties as executive vice president by the Board for personal failings and Farriba, who by that time had authored a more detailed merger plan as general manager, was elevated to the executive VP post.[124]

Regardless, it was the start of external wrangling that would go on for almost 14 years between the Atlanta-based and Louisville-based bureaus before their merger finally did take place at approximately the same time as Womack's retirement. In between, neither staff ever rested easy. Amidst the heightened uncertainty brought on by deregulation, which officially started with the Motor Carriers Act of 1980, but was actually in the works by 1977, major personal expenditures like cars or houses were largely not acted upon by leadership or the rank-and-file of either bureau. While maintaining relations, at least on the surface, competition among all bureaus was on the rise as they all searched for survival tactics and red flags were everywhere when it came to the two southern bureau staffs that had much in common but much more at stake.[125]

As confirmed in the previous chapter, CSA had found what appeared a winning niche with technology. On the other hand, the Louisville bureau had somewhat irrationally invested in printing equipment, owning one of the Derby City's largest print shops with large web presses and employing around 100 people. That would necessitate taking outside jobs just to keep those presses running.[126]

"With its computer/technology efforts and the size of its print shop, CSA obviously had the much larger portfolio at that time," Slaton emphasized. "By the same token, SMC had the much larger and healthier carrier membership and better financial picture. The key was obviously to somehow save the best of both organizations. What the leadership of both organizations knew was that the best of both worlds, if it could be achieved, was to blend CSA's technology savvy with SMC's membership and better business practices. Everyone was trying to achieve synergy."[127]

Into this effort, Farriba, with the backing of the SMC Board, took the previously ICC approved bylaws of both bureaus and began to develop his plan. "First I wanted to see if I could merge the bylaws into one coherent document that could withstand ICC scrutiny and win approval," he recalled.

At least twice, filings were made and rejected by the ICC with resulting requests that they be "re-worked," and from 1977 through 1982, "almost five years," merger efforts "languished" in Washington, D.C., before being withdrawn or dropped. Confirmation that these rejections were to be expected came from legal representation in the D. C. area as early as January 1978.[128] "All the while, our carrier members were voicing support and loyalty was building," Farriba said. "We had a Board that liked what we were doing and, I don't mind saying, they liked me. We had always tried to understand and address our carriers' needs. At the same time, I think there was residual animosity towards CSA for what Womack had tried even though 90 percent of the (southern) carriers did business with both. Personalities were involved. Whereas we continued to say leave well enough alone, they had attempted to force things."

From the beginning, Farriba's plans called for leaving certain things in Atlanta and certain things in Louisville. "By the early 1980s, every bureau had done some software development and we were all competing in that area to some extent. We knew what CSA had and we knew they were better, but we also felt good about our management and salaries, which were much less than theirs, and we knew their print shop situation was unsustainable," he related.

Eventually in those same early '80s, talks were held between the two with printing remaining a big issue. "That was the one big hang-up," Farriba confirmed. "He (Womack) was already soliciting for commercial printing business and wanted to continue their print shop. At the same time, I wanted to maintain what we had for printing because I knew theirs couldn't last. In fact, we had knowledge of the fact they were reissuing their tariff books sooner than necessary, whether they had changes or not. That was a way bureaus could make extra money, but it was a practice that wasn't fair to carriers or shippers. Such decisions, we felt, were obviously precipitated by more expenses than they had revenue."

Nevertheless, "we couldn't come to an agreement," Farriba confirmed, and actual merger talks between the two bureaus were dropped in 1984. "It was removed from the Boards' agendas and I was relieved when the talks were dropped, but the idea was never far from the carriers' minds and with Board members changing on both sides, a motion to renew consideration for a merger was introduced with our Board (SMC) in 1987. A letter to that effect was sent by our president, Glenn Brown of Yellow Freight, to their president, Tony Pope of Roadway Express," he added.[129]

As previously noted, that was about the same time as Womack's announcement of his retirement intentions and almost 13 years after what had appeared to be his takeover bid.[130] Then, on January 12, 1988, at the end of an SMC Board of Governors meeting at the Colony Square Hotel in Atlanta, the meeting minutes had been officially closed and everyone was about to adjourn, when Gene West, an industry giant and obviously influential Board member from Consolidated Freightways, slammed his fist on the table and shouted, "God damn it, let's merge these bureaus!"

Immediately and with no discussion, like soldiers obeying a direct order, everyone returned to their seats, the minutes were re-opened, and the meeting resumed with West making the fateful motion that would ultimately result in approval by both Boards for the merger of the two associations. Over the next five months, more meetings, reports, resolutions, proposals, and notices followed, but with West leading the way, it was ultimately agreed that Southern Motor Carriers, Atlanta's branch of the original motor carrier bureau structure and the enduring association that would eventually become

SMC³ 15 years later, would be the surviving identity.[131] On June 1, 1988, the merger was ratified and before that month was over, appropriate documents were again filed with the ICC, which granted approval on March 24, 1989.[132] On June 6 of that year, the long anticipated merger was finally official.[133]

Actually, according to Farriba, other mergers with other bureaus were also explored by SMC after the final, successful absorption of CSA. The Central States and Middle Atlantic bureaus were two he indicated were approached and, in fact, Middlewest Motor Freight did merge with Central States Motor Freight in early 1993.[134] Today, on a far smaller scale than SMC³, Middlewest Motor Freight of Kansas City, Missouri, is the only other former collective ratemaking bureau offering its own rate formulating software – a product called MARS.[135]

Chapter eight
Labor Pains Of Merger

As one of the youngest and newest members of the Central and Southern rate bureau staff, Beach can remember "feeling terrible" about "old-timers" being laid off after the merger with SMC was announced. As would have been the case with any bureau, the long-standing CSA Standing Rate Committee and Research Department were two of the obviously over-lapping divisions of the merging bureaus that were among the first to go when the Louisville branch of the collective ratemaking business was suddenly downgraded. Of necessity, there would be many others.

"It was hard to accept because we (CSA) had always thought with what we brought to the table (technology), we shouldn't lose out to Atlanta (SMC)," Beach added when recalling news of the merger. "I mean, besides being bigger, what did they (SMC) offer? Maybe that sounds like sour grapes or false hope, but it's how we felt at the time."[136]

Perhaps reliving that period more objectively, Owen admitted, "Now we had always wished we had the core group of carriers that SMC enjoyed and when the two Boards finally got around to merging, maybe that was the over-riding factor in their decision which way to lean. We still had ongoing contracts with Central States and Niagara, but they (SMC) were a lot bigger and I guess had more loyalty and clout. None of that stopped us from viewing Jack (Middleton) as a hatchet man at the time."[137]

No job for the faint of heart, in point of fact, was the role Farriba thrust upon his future successor when the merger became official in 1989. Under Middleton's leadership, consolidation teams were formed in Atlanta and CSA was down-sized as the two bureaus reluctantly went about the stressful business of becoming one. Actually, the CSA staff expected to be entirely closed down and for about 18 months feelings were admittedly ugly.

"To us, it felt like a hostile takeover," Beach remembered before Middleton acknowledged, "We had no experience with what we were doing and we did a poor job with that merger. We really did. Looking back there are things that could have been handled differently. I'm sure such things as people losing jobs is never fun, but I'm also sure larger corporations that have experience with mergers are better at it than we were."[138]

Although many in Louisville had still not come to terms with the merger, they had by the time CSA's massive print shop was dismantled and its staff let go. Among its auctioned items on March 1, 1990, were heavy duty offset presses, strapping machines, a paper jogger, drill presses, collating machines, furniture and fixtures, and a myriad of supplies such as giant paper rolls, inks, and stitching material, air compressors and binders - even a company car. In fact, one auction wasn't enough; it took two.[139] "With the publication of tariffs gone from day one (of the merger), there was simply no way to justify that print shop," Owen acknowledged. The two Boards were finally consolidated in 1990, and after that, people were let go gradually in several waves with the final layoffs coming in 1993. Owen also remembered that as the year Farriba advised him a profit must be made in order to continue the Louisville office at all - the obvious way being further development and marketing of the new technology.[140]

Ultimately just over 20 staffers would remain from what had been a CSA staff of approximately 150 since the late 1930s, necessitating a search and move to smaller quarters, and the adjustment from longtime property owner to what Middleton termed "an anchor tenant" in nearby, leased office space. That, in turn, led to the sale of the previous CSA headquarters, a transaction made more difficult by the need to rectify asbestos problems in that building before any sale could be consummated.[141]

Initially, before all the layoffs were concluded, there was also a duplication of efforts. It was almost as if the bureaus were competing entities though suddenly under the same umbrella. Sales staffs in both Louisville and Atlanta continued to do their jobs as usual although often pitted against each other behind the scenes by common clients anxious to take advantage for "the best deal" they could get given the dual situation. In lieu of direct coordination between the two staffs, an overall resident manager was established in Louisville to simply oversee basic work ethics like punctuality, proper attire, comportment, and the like.

Not until the theory of cross management was established were the growing pains of rivalry and duplication largely eliminated. According to Beach, "Cross management with established department managers in one place or the other directly overseeing people in both got us away from the 'we and them' that had been plaguing joint operations. Once we convinced Jack of the need for such a setup, things went a lot smoother, but it took awhile to get there."[142]

Meanwhile, the trucking industry remained what Owen termed, "One of the least technology-driven industries in the world in those days." He even recalled being asked many times to assist one carrier or another in just getting new personal computers set up – literally, "with the computer still in the box, they were asking, 'can you help us?'"

Despite this reluctance, continued development of the by-then SMC software initiatives continued. "We were developing software that had to be leading edge and we all knew it, but we were also still supporting our old stuff a lot longer than we should have been," Owen admitted. Beach also commented, "We would have liked to gradually eliminate our support of the older systems, but I can remember many times Charlie had to be out of the office doing tech support. He made many trips to dozens and dozens of different carrier members helping them with basics."[143]

Eventually, only the sales and technology components remained in Louisville with the sales part represented solely in the person of Slaton, who remained the key go-between with the developing carrier and shipper world when it came to CzarLite and the rest of SMC's emerging rate-producing software. Recognizing this, Farriba had set an early course to move Slaton from Louisville to Atlanta, but had been rebuffed. An Indiana native, Slaton obviously enjoyed his location in Louisville, just across the Ohio River from his native state, and had no desire to move southward as long as the Kentucky office remained an option, especially if it entailed being subordinate to any sales and/or marketing personnel already in Atlanta.

Except for the technology, however, with all other operations clearly based at the southernmost location by 1994-95, including sales and marketing on an increasing basis, the importance of Slaton's transfer became ever more apparent, drawing the personal attention of Middleton as GM. "I went to Vernon and asked if he minded me trying my hand in renewing the talks with Danny," Middleton remembered. "He said no, but that he was pretty sure Danny was entrenched in Louisville and would never seriously consider the move. But it was definitely worth another try, so I renewed talks and kept them going despite being turned down myself, at least once. I knew Danny was close to the group up there, so I spent a lot of time showing him what we were dealing with and why the move made sense. I told him I was closing Sales in Louisville, but I also assured him he would never be subordinate to anyone in Sales in Atlanta and he finally relented and began to accept our goal for one, consolidated Sales team. His coming to Atlanta was another big piece in the merger puzzle."[144]

At the same time, it also seemed another blow to the already damaged psyche in Louisville. "When Danny Slaton agreed to move to Atlanta, I thought we were really down the tubes," Beach admitted. "That's when Charlie and I really had to be cheerleaders to try and keep spirits up."[145]

And actually, Farriba and Middleton had been receiving questions from their own, consolidated Board of Governors

SMC³ Leadership Through the Years

W. M. Miller (1938-1964)

Bill Brown (1965-1975)

L. Vernon Farriba (1976-1996)

Jack E. Middleton (1996-2016)

Andrew C. Slusher (2016-)

Originally called general manager and later executive vice president, the position of chief executive officer at SMC³ has evolved to where that person is now known as president, a title previously reserved for the head of the organization's Board (now chairman).

The host for hundreds of meetings and events during its eight decades of service to the transportation industry, this dinner on September 24, 1937 was one of the first - a major gala at the no-longer existent Hotel Ansley in the Fairlie-Poplar District of Downtown Atlanta.

One of the early trucking pioneers in the South, W. W. Estes began his career hauling livestock to market in the Northeast before founding one of the leading LTL companies in Richmond, Virginia, Estes Express – still recognized nationwide by its "Big E" logo. *(Courtesy Estes Express Lines)*

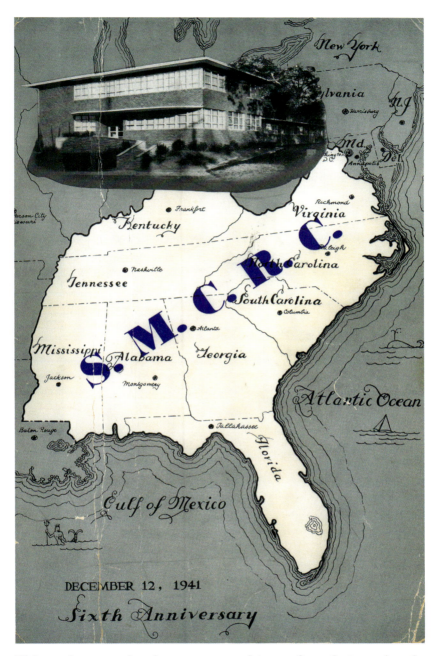

This early promotional map was used to confirm that carriers in nine southeastern states had banded together to conduct motor freight collective ratemaking under the umbrella of the ICC-approved Southern Motor Carriers Rate Conference.

In 1941, the early pioneers of SMC³ broke ground on the first of three headquarters the association would build in the Atlanta area. This original building was at 873 Spring Street.

A giant of the motor freight industry for 75 years and known for its well-organized, union workforce (Teamsters), Yellow Freight was founded by A. J. Harrell, shown here beside one of his early "big rigs." In 1999, Yellow Freight merged with Roadway, forming YRC. *(Courtesy Yellow Roadway Corporation)*

This 1950s-era photo of the Southern Motor Carriers Executive Staff shows W. M. Miller (behind desk) meeting with Ruth Dial, Archie Culbreth, Ruben Crimm, Bob Steed, Fred Lee, Alex Henslee, and John Shumate. Miller brought railroad bureau experience to his job as executive vice president.

W. M. Miller (left), SMC^3's first chief executive officer, was obviously all smiles upon receiving this American Trucking Association National Freight Council certificate of merit from J. L. Hopkins during the 1950s, one of many industry accolades the organization has received through the years.

Every motor freight collective ratemaking bureau in the country had its Standing Rate Committee. When this photo was taken in 1958, Southern Motor Carriers' four-man SRC included Claude Adams, Bob Hopkins, Emory Moss and Fred Lee.

The Rate Department at Southern Motor Carriers was a busy and obviously a very organized place, as this late 1950s photograph clearly illustrates.

SMC³'s second home was Midtown Atlanta. The prestigious address was 1307 Peachtree Street - across the street from Atlanta's High Museum of Art.

The influence of trucking in the South is illustrated by this early 1960s photo of former Tennessee Governor Bill Clement addressing a gathering of carrier executives in Chattanooga, Tennessee. Collectively operating through Southern Motor Carriers, the major carrier companies located in the South would remain among the most successful in the country.

Known as the Board of Governors during bureau days, when nine Southeastern states had one representative each among the Southern Motor Carrier's 10-man leadership group, this 1965 Board included one of the most influential members in SMC³ history - Overnite Transportation's Harwood Cochrane (front left) - as well as SMC Executive VP Bill Brown (5th from left, back row).

SUPPLEMENT 4

TO

TARIFF 8-G

MF-ICC 1435

Cancels Supplement 3 (For additional cancellation, see Page 2)
Supplements 2 and 4 contain all changes

SOUTHERN MOTOR CARRIERS RATE CONFERENCE, AGENT

LOCAL, JOINT, PROPORTIONAL, EXPORT AND IMPORT COMMODITY RATES

ALSO
DISTANCE OR MILEAGE COMMODITY RATES (See Section 2)
VIA
ALL MOTOR, MOTOR-RAIL, RAIL-MOTOR, MOTOR-RAIL-MOTOR AND RAIL-MOTOR-RAIL ROUTES

FROM POINTS IN		TO POINTS IN	
ALABAMA ARKANSAS (Helena and West Helena, only) FLORIDA GEORGIA KENTUCKY	LOUISIANA (Southeastern) MISSISSIPPI NORTH CAROLINA SOUTH CAROLINA TENNESSEE VIRGINIA (Southern)	CONNECTICUT DELAWARE DISTRICT OF COLUMBIA MAINE MARYLAND MASSACHUSETTS NEW HAMPSHIRE	NEW JERSEY NEW YORK OHIO (Eastern) PENNSYLVANIA RHODE ISLAND VERMONT VIRGINIA (Eastern) WEST VIRGINIA (Northern)

This tariff applies only on Interstate traffic

SOUTH-EAST COMMODITY TARIFF

For reference to governing classification and other publications, see Item 130

ISSUED FEBRUARY 24, 1967 **EFFECTIVE APRIL 7, 1967**
(Except as otherwise provided herein)

ISSUED BY

L. VERNON FARRIBA, Chief of Tariff Bureau,
1307 PEACHTREE STREET, N.E.
POST OFFICE BOX 7347, STATION C,
ATLANTA, GEORGIA, 30309

Communications regarding rates and other provisions published herein should be addressed to the traffic officials of the carriers parties to this tariff

(2200)   0306—THE STEIN PRINTING CO., ATLANTA, GA.   (Printed in U.S.A.)

The front of this South-East Commodity Tariff issued while Vernon Farriba was chief of tariff at Southern Motor Carriers in 1967 is illustrative of the thousands of collectively formulated and published rates released on a continuous basis during bureau days.

In 1978, Vernon Farriba of Southern Motor Carriers was one of several industry executives subpoenaed by Edward Kennedy's Senate Transportation and Infrastructure Committee to testify on deregulation. Seated with Farriba (left) in this Washington, D.C., photo was Sam Herold of the Middle Atlantic Conference and Jim Harkins of the National Motor Freight Association.

Senator Kennedy, visible in the upper left corner of this photo, later penned a letter commending Farriba (seated center and leaning forward) on his very candid contribution at the D.C. hearing.

EDWARD M. KENNEDY
MASSACHUSETTS

United States Senate
WASHINGTON, D.C. 20510

6 April 1978

Mr. L. Vernon Farriba
Southern Motor Carriers Rate Conference
Post Office Box 7219
Atlanta, Georgia 30309

Dear Mr. Farriba:

I wanted to let you know how much I appreciated your appearance at our hearings on collective ratemaking in the freight motor carrier industry. Your testimony was very helpful to us, and I am sure we will be calling on you for advice and assistance as we continue our examination of this important issue.

Once again, thank you for taking the time to be with us.

Best personal regards.

Sincerely,

Edward M. Kennedy

Following his testimony at the 1978 Senate hearings dealing with motor freight issues, Vernon Farriba received this letter from Edward Kennedy acknowledging his valuable contribution during the D.C. proceedings.

Pictured alongside stacks of collectively developed rate tariffs, Vernon Farriba was general manager and executive vice president of the Southern Motor Carriers Rate Conference when it merged with the Central and Southern Tariff Association. This 1982 picture was featured in the Business Section of the *Atlanta Constitution (courtesy AJC and Associated Press).*

Dan Acker, shown here during his earliest days at SMC³, and his team were initially laid off. Acker was later brought back through the efforts of Jack Middleton because of his unique ability to translate the motor freight pricing process.

The father of the CZAR and CzarLite family of pricing software that paved the way for SMC³'s industry leadership into the new century, Charlie Owen was the recognized leader of the Louisville-based technicians responsible for computerizing motor freight rates in the late 1980s.

LIMITED OFFER

Introducing *CZAR*-Lite.

IDENTIFICATION NO. _____

EASY AFFORDABLE NATIONWIDE RATING WITH ACTUAL BUREAU RATES.

CZAR-Lite could easily change the way you think about motor carrier rates. It is competitive with individual carrier diskettes for analysis, rate quotes, charge backs, carrier negotiations and special traffic department projects.

CZAR-Lite was designed to be the first truly affordable national rating system suitable for mass distribution. Our unique data base design allowed us to compact all the information needed for five-digit rating accuracy on a dual-floppy diskette microcomputer system. This data base includes 16 tariffs from the 10 major motor carrier tariff bureaus.

CZAR-Lite basing matrix and rate base numbers will address themselves to any level of bureau based motor carrier rates. With our limited release offer we are issuing the market base level of LTL class rates effective December 1, 1987. These rates are taken from the Bureau Tariffs and Section Numbers listed.

CZAR *Lite*

NATIONWIDE .... Rates from anywhere to anywhere.
COMPACT .... Works on dual floppy or hard disk computers.
FAST .... Instantaneous look-ups and rate calculations.
AUTOMATIC ...... Selects proper bureau, tariff authority and rate base number by five-digit zip code pair.
ACCURATE .... Our test of 2,500 freight bills showed CZAR-Lite was 99% accurate. (Test report available)
SIMPLE .... Easy to install and operate. Takes less than five minutes to install, less than thirty minutes to learn.
SUPPORTED ...... Your system is supported by our staff experts and a toll free CZAR Watts Line.

TERRITORY CODES AND APPLICABLE BUREAU TARIFF

BUREAU	TARIFF #	SECTION #
Central States	CMB 347	6
	CMB 575	6
Central and Southern	CSA 501	4
Eastern Central	ECA 531,532 or 533	5
Middle Atlantic	MAC 500 or 515	4
	MAC 308	4
Middlewest	MWB 550	3
New England	NEB 599	3E
Niagara Frontier	NFB 362	6
Pacific Inland	PIN 500	7
Rocky Mountain	RMB 583	4
Southern Conference	SMC 500 and 585	1
	SMC 585	3
	SMC 585	4

For Immediate Service Call:
1-800-272-3425 / (502) 636-3361

CZAR-LITE CERTIFICATE

☐ **YES, PLEASE SEND ME CZAR-Lite FOR THE LIMITED RELEASE PRICE OF $99.**

☐ YES, Enclose the free listing of the top 100 carriers and their Independent Action level in bureau rate scales.
☐ My check is enclosed. For VISA or MASTERCHARGE call 1-800-272-3425
☐ Bill my company, I understand that this method of Billing will require a $10 administrative handling charge.

NAME _____ COMPANY _____
ADDRESS _____ TELEPHONE ( ) _____
CITY _____ STATE _____ ZIP _____

LICENSE AGREEMENT: I understand that CZAR-Lite is the property of Central and Southern Motor Freight Tariff Association and agree that I will not duplicate and give away or sell copies of the program and data without a licensing agreement with CSA. I further understand that CSA limits its warranty on CZAR-Lite and shall not be responsible for any consequential, incidental or contingent damages incurred through its use. Further I understand that CZAR-Lite may be used only as an aid in interpreting the class rate portions of the tariffs and section numbers listed; that CZAR-Lite does not offer aid in tariff interpretation concerning carrier participation, routing or rules and that the lawfully applicable rate on any shipment will be determined by the provision of such tariffs.

SIGNATURE: _____, DATE _____, IDENT. # _____

The original CZAR-Lite promotional sales piece, some of which is shown here, was an instant success with its special introductory offer for revolutionary new rate-producing software. Carrier response to the mass mailing was immediate and ongoing for weeks.

Along with Charlie Owen, Julie Beach and Danny Slaton were mainstays of bureau operations in Louisville, Kentucky at the time of the merger of CSA with SMC, and both would remain mainstays once the combined organization became known as SMC[3].

Effectively passing the torch at SMC³, Vernon Farriba (right) receives a congratulatory handshake from his hand-picked successor, Jack Middleton, at his retirement celebration in 1996.

When SMC³ instituted education as part of its trilogy of service along with technology and data in 1996, its first group of conference speakers included Carleton Bailey of the Transportation Brokers Association, Clyde Hart of the U.S. Department of Transportation, and Washington-based, transportation legal expert John Bagileo, just beginning his long association with the organization.

In 1999, SMC[3] moved its headquarters to the Atlanta suburb of Peachtree City. This was an early artist rendering of the impressive new three-story home that would become known as Commerce Center.

Jack Brooks, the smiling young man with the dark hair in the foreground of this early bureau era photo, was among those who had to make choices when SMC³ moved from Midtown Atlanta to Peachtree City. His decision to remain with the organization resulted in a record-setting 51-plus year career.

Pictured with Jack Middleton (right) during groundbreaking ceremonies at Peachtree City in 1999, Paul Weaver of Watkins Motor Lines, was instrumental in maintaining an additional SMC^3 office in Louisville after the merger with CSA. Middleton (also shown speaking) oversaw the merger and move from Midtown Atlanta to its southern suburbs.

Visionary leader Jack Middleton, who introduced educational conferences to the SMC³ agenda in 1996, is pictured alongside Bill Zollars, renowned CEO of YRC Worldwide and the speaker credited with helping SMC³ conferences "turn the corner" through his appearance at both the winter and summer meetings of 2005.

Now executive vice president and COO, Danny Slaton, shown here engaged in conversation with one of the 400-plus transportation professionals who regularly attend SMC³ conferences, played a leading role in the industry's transition from collective ratemaking to technology-based pricing.

Respected veterans of SMC³'s bureau days, Vernon Farriba, Dean Stowers, and Leajar Brooks were among the pioneers who made collective ratemaking a smooth operation in the South. They all still frequently return for conferences and retiree functions.

With technology and data as keys to SMC³'s survival, success, and service, the server rooms in both Peachtree City and Louisville are literally two beating hearts of motor freight pricing.

Typical of the big stage and expert panels SMC³ routinely features at twice annual conferences, this scene from Jump Start 2015 took place at the Loews Hotel in Atlanta.

Standout entertainment is now a staple of SMC[3] conferences, as illustrated by Elton John impersonator Craig Meyer at the 2015 Connections summer conference in San Diego.

John Rader, whose leadership of the Industry and Educational Services program was instrumental in the continued development of SMC^3 conferences in the early 2000s, is pictured while in his master of ceremonies role portraying an early American patriot. Rader credited themed conferences like this one in Boston with helping attendance rise throughout his decade at the I&ES helm.

David Knight, an SMC³ senior vice-president and CIO, shared this moment with college football coaching legend Lou Holtz during the 2014 winter conference in Atlanta. Knight, who oversees all technology and program development, introduced Holtz, who was the conference keynote speaker.

Traditionally composed of LTL carrier leaders, and SMC[3] executives, the January, 2015 SMC[3] Board included (first row) John Bagileo, Jack Middleton, Andrew Slusher, and Russell Garrett; (second row) Rick Bowden, Rob Estes, Ken Burroughs, David Sexton, Danny Slaton, and Paul Weaver; (third row) Brent Holliday, Reid Dove, Larry Kerr, and Bill Reed; (fourth row) Steve Gast, Tommy Hodges, and Mark Davis. With the advent of many more shippers and logistics providers among its clients, that traditional makeup is changing. The first non-carrier member was added in June, 2015.

Led by new leaders like Tom Swinson (above) in I&ES and Andrew Slusher as president, SMC³ is still well positioned to address the changing transportation landscape as it approaches a century of service.

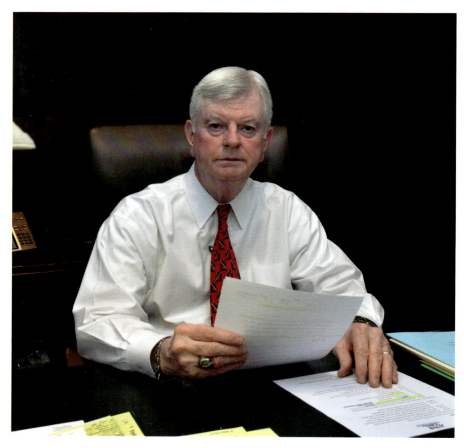

The year 2016 marked the end of Jack Middleton's tenure as CEO of SMC³ – two decades of growth and change that revolutionized motor freight pricing. As outgoing chairman of the SMC³ Board, Ken Burroughs said, "SMC³ is the only former rate bureau that not only survived, but also evolved into the leading provider of supply chain technology and on-going education in the industry. This would not have happened without the transformative vision and leadership of Jack Middleton. The Board of Directors has been extremely proud of Jack's leadership and guidance."

about why everything was taking so long and not already located in Atlanta? "One Board member even went so far as to tell me I should let them (Louisville staff) know this is how it is going to be 'and to not let the door hit them in the ass on their way out,'" Middleton acknowledged. "But I had gotten to know the remaining staff up there, the people like Charlie, Julie, and Danny who had created the technology we would be taking into a new era of motor freight pricing, and I knew we still needed them. In fact, during a staff meeting up there, I had already assured them that I was not going to close what remained of the Louisville office and if the Board ever directed me to do so, I would resign. The majority of the Board was in favor of closing the Louisville office and even after a couple of years, it would still come up. To a certain extent, you couldn't blame them. As CEOs themselves, they were looking at it from the bottom line perspective and thus their question, 'why do you need offices in two places?' Thankfully, the leader of our Board at the time, Paul Weaver of Watkins Motor Lines in Florida, had done a lot of work with the Louisville staff through the years and respected my position. Paul really helped me quell that recurring theme."[146]

Justification for that decision quickly became available when it became necessary to start moving all computer products and services into the new, Windows-based system for PCs. At first, no one on staff had experience with Windows, but that didn't stop the technology from continuing to evolve. "It evolved in a different form and with changed accessibility, and it was bound to keep evolving," Owen stated. "Meanwhile, we had different products coming along and different ways for people to access those products through such things as number of computer hits and either monthly or annual licensing." Both were to provide huge benefits.[147]

Those benefits were apparently evident even the first year. According to a section authored by Farriba in the 1989 annual report, which was published 18 months after the merger, expenses were expected to be down by $2 million, "a direct savings to the carriers and their shipper subscribers." That was "in addition to the savings resulting from the elimination of duplicate activities."[148] The internal storm finally passed and their organization stabilized, Farriba and Middleton, along with the rest of the industry, next turned their attention to the rapidly changing external transportation landscape.

Chapter nine
Regulation Reminiscing

Federal regulation and states' rights may sound like opposite ends of the transportation spectrum, but deregulation made for strange bedfellows in the 1980s and '90s. While the earlier bureau era of collective ratemaking had its detractors, especially when it came to the largest shippers clamoring for a more laissez-faire approach and open competition among carriers, the old adage of "be careful what you wish for" seemed appropriate once deregulation had taken hold.

A 1983 article by Drexel University Professor Jerold Muskin in the January *Transportation Quarterly* even foretold that eventuality. In it, he concluded:

> "While government intervention may be costly to administer and may bring about certain inefficiencies, free market determination of infrastructure capacity and quality levels may be even more costly in terms of the direct costs to the participants and, more significantly, may impose future costs and fairness violations on the community that are heavier than direct costs."[149]

In other words, deregulation would not go smoothly. Belzer's book, *Sweatshops On Wheels,* lends itself to a precise look at this emerging dilemma in the history of motor freight. Bureaus like SMC had obviously been a key component of the industry's regulated structure since 1935 and by the 1970s, government policy had become focused on dismantling regulation, "appealing to values intrinsic to the

American psyche: liberty over control, individualism over community." These were the core principals among the nation's major financial institutions and there's little doubt those same institutions dominated marketplace debate.

Along with this deregulation concept, however, this "unfettered competition," came "social and economic costs." Although the previous system of regulation had promoted designated but often illogical routes, it had also stabilized the infant industry by addressing the interrelated problems of railroads, carriers, shippers, and the general public. It even provided a forum for labor issues.[150]

Suddenly, this time-tested trucking landscape saw its proven rules of the road and the old ICC forced to the curb. New strategies of divide and conquer just as suddenly emerged. It was competition that would further divide LTL from truckload.

As Belzer emphasized, "Both carriers and their employees lost as a result of deregulation, as average return for general commodity freight eroded and wages dropped substantially." The "deregulation of trucking converted middle-class jobs with reasonable benefits and retirement possibilities into low-wage jobs unlikely to provide career employment and no retirement benefits."[151]

A Nashville-based truck driver for Yellow Freight for 20 years and a Teamster for all 35 of his driving career, Tommy Gammons never experienced a downturn in wages or benefits before retirement in 1994, but he did witness the consolidations (or takeovers) that occurred in the trucking business, including four name changes just among the carriers he worked for before Yellow. "I lucked out by being union in all the places I worked. I had chances to go with newer shops that weren't union, some of whom were started by friends of mine, but I always said I was gonna ride the union ship until it sunk and I've always been glad I did," he reminisced. "When deregulation came and opened up all the routes, I can remember a lot of guys that lost their jobs and had virtually no retirement. I was fortunate to not only be union, but to also be with one of the bigger carriers."[152]

Under the old system of ICC-sanctioned rate bureaus and designated routes, competition had been largely limited to level of service. Legislation had exempted the bureaus and their carrier members from antitrust laws, and shippers generally relied on different carriers to ensure all their traffic needs. In fact, without "blanket, national coverage," most carriers still relied on mostly local or regional routes and bureau tariffs created a means whereby partnering carriers could share freight and combine rates through interline shipments. For the most part, trucking companies viewed the railroads as their greatest competition, not other truck lines.

Under the new, deregulated system, there was free entry into the marketplace, inspiring hundreds of overnight startups and immediate access to all routes, which sharply curtailed orderly ratemaking and encouraged many carriers, especially the larger ones, to charge "discriminatory prices" that amounted to discounts for their volume customers. Needless to say, with those discount practices and so many more carriers, "competition became intense."

Just as in other industries, deregulation opened every market to free entry. It basically "withdrew rate regulatory authority from the bureaus," caused carriers to "discriminate when accepting or rejecting freight" based on their particular business strategy, and allowed "rates at whatever the market could bear." Again, according to Belzer, "Carriers began to cut each other's throats by discounting broadly." And with more forced specialization – either LTL or truckload – there's no doubt LTL carriers suffered the most.[153]

As late as mid-1992, in a commentary written for the trade publication *Traffic World,* Fritz Kahn wrote:

> "A laissez-faire ICC has not involved itself with regulating motor carrier rates, deeming them best left to the workings of the marketplace. Indeed, the agency has encouraged truckers to offer discounts and other forms of innovative pricing techniques. (This) arrangement worked perfectly so long as truckers were

able to make some money. As some carriers became pressed for profits, however, they offered even greater rate reductions in an effort to enlarge their market shares, often at below-compensatory levels, and their collapse (as a result) became inevitable."

That same article indicated "hundreds of truckers" had gone into bankruptcy. Also, audits uncovered hundreds of discrepancies between charges the carriers had assessed in trying to get (and stay) ahead of their newfound competition and what previously established ICC tariffs indicated they should have charged. These audits also led to literally thousands of undercharge claims against unsuspecting shippers after the fact, especially when the Supreme Court "affirmed the validity" of such claims in its 1990 Maislin decision.[154]

Dan Acker, a former aviation electronics worker, came to work for SMC in the Costing Department in 1978, just before deregulation, and remembered well that no discounts were given prior to 1982. "Carriers could give lower rates, but they had to have ICC approval and it had to be done within established time frames," he said. "Prior to 1980, they had to charge class rates. Those were the highest that could be charged. But in the early '80s, carriers began publishing specific rates. At SMC, we still published the class rates, but also exceptions through independent announcements."

He also remembered a GRC Meeting in 1981, when the same Harwood Cochrane who had entered the initial resolution for the merger of SMC and CSA in 1975, spoke out about how tired he was of "messing with all this stuff," meaning the class rates, and how his company, Overnite, was going to give 10 percent discounts across the board. "As far as we were concerned at SMC, that started the percentage discount approach, especially by the larger LTL carriers," Acker recalled.

In the tariff books, all that had to be entered to show a carrier discount was one additional sentence, but as suddenly-emerging carrier marketing departments also got involved, bigger and bigger discounts became prevalent. "It was a form of rate manipulation," Acker maintained. "It was a means of showing discounts of up to six or even eight percent and gradually the old carrier traffic departments were displaced by marketing people. Shippers wanted a set of rates – period – and, of course (as previously discussed), that was the genesis of what became CzarLite."[155]

According to a June 1982 article in the Business Section of the *Atlanta Constitution* headlined "Do Trucks Need Ratemakers?" the advantages of collective ratemaking made LTL carriers and major shippers "a coalition" of sorts. Both groups couldn't help but worry that "free-market philosophies in a complex industry" like theirs might "lapse into chaos" without the collectively established rates to rely on. Without collective rates, many felt small shippers would lose any chance to negotiate. To address such concerns a study was conducted by the Motor Carrier Ratemaking Commission, for which its executive director, Larry Darby, rationalized:

"There's a theory of the marketplace and a theory of regulation. Everyone subscribes to one or the other in glowing terms. We're trying to go through the spectrum of arguments and see what's supported and what's not. But the only real test of the industry with or without collective ratemaking is to go without it and see what happens."[156]

It was during that same let's-give-it-a-try period, that Acker began compiling an annual record of how many LTL carriers were currently doing business. In 1979, when everyone figured deregulation was on the way but before it became official, there were approximately 450 LTL carriers in the U.S. By 1990, just 11 years later, that original LTL number had dropped precipitously to about 50.

Eight years earlier, again in '82, another *Traffic World* commentary by Kurt Freedlund actually spoke to that trend. In it Freedlund stated:

"It may be true that thousands of new trucking companies have been founded creating jobs, but what of the nearly 2,000 trucking companies per year which have gone bankrupt? Of the 30 largest trucking firms in the United States in 1979, only seven remain. What occurred was that while the number of carriers doubled (as the result of deregulation), the amount of freight to be hauled remained basically the same (and) this lopsidedness in the supply and demand created major price wars resulting in non-compensatory rates by the carriers. In such an environment, it (was) only a matter of time before companies must close their doors."

Freedlund, a chief transportation attorney for the Illinois Commerce Commission, also confirmed that "big shippers, the loudest voices demanding deregulation," were the ones who benefitted most from the proliferation of trucking discounts. His term for the discounts was "price wars." As for the losers in deregulation, he broke it down this way:

"1} The small and rural shippers who cannot find reliable trucking service or when they do, end up paying (for) the carriers' losses resulting from the discounts given the big shippers. 2} The carriers who find themselves in price wars for the limited (or unchanged) amount of freight. 3} The American public, which once again must bear the cost of unemployment, bankruptcies, debt, and deteriorated safety."[157]

At the same time, discounts and their residual issues were not the only motor freight malady brought on by interstate deregulation. In fact, states' rights - that term so often connected to limiting federal intervention - came into play in the motor freight business as a result of the public service commissions in 44 states still claiming intrastate authority over freight and freight rates within their borders. That is until Congress acknowledged and mandated "intrastate economic deregulation in January 1995."

Again according to Belzer, that legislation was primarily the result of a dispute between UPS and Federal Express. Apparently, with FedEx originally considered an "air taxi" or "air express service," that special status, which was not subject to the Motor Carrier Act of 1980, all changed as the company began to use trucks, transforming itself into a general freight carrier. Obviously UPS, classified as a motor carrier from the beginning, was subject to very different rules, which all came to a head in California. That's where UPS, as the result of its motor carrier status, found itself regulated by that state's public utilities commission and at a very competitive disadvantage.

Once this dispute between up-and-coming transportation heavyweights landed in the courts, leadership from the still-regulated states mounted campaigns to show their constituencies were being subjected to economic disadvantage, while unregulated state leaders complained that the regulated states were hindering "the free flow of commerce." As a result of being caught in these "crosshairs," the days of intrastate regulation were numbered and ultimately ended in 1995.[158]

Less than three years prior, in October of 1992, another *Traffic World* "Special Report" had illustrated why this untenable situation was bound to happen. In it, Mark Solomon posed the dilemma:

> "When Congress passed landmark bills in 1980, deregulating interstate surface transportation, many people naturally assumed that similar freedoms on the intrastate level would soon follow. So they sat back and waited. Twelve years later, they are still waiting."

This "last frontier in the deregulation odyssey" was debated by deregulators claiming states' rights protected "privileged cartels" of local truckers who "inflated the nation's freight tab." At the same time, opponents argued that deregulation would flood their highways with thousands of new truckers, further eroding infrastructure, jeopardizing safety, and costing the livelihood of small and rural carriers who wouldn't survive if forced to do without the high rate protection of their in-state regulations.[159] As with the ICC's interstate regulation, however, it was the unified voice of shippers that eventually held sway; shippers outraged by the higher intrastate rates found in some states than in others - rates they finally demanded go away. The UPS-FedEx dispute also marked the final straw for the ICC, which saw its remaining responsibilities distributed among other agencies while it was being "sun-setted."[160]

As for the specific history of SMC^3, there was at least one time when states' rights rates rode to the rescue. It began in 1984 when the U.S. government claimed the bureau was violating terms of the Sherman Antitrust Act by its collective ratemaking actions within the borders of four states, North Carolina, Tennessee, Georgia, and Mississippi. The case, Southern Motor Carriers Rate Conference, Inc., vs. United States, opened in the 11th Circuit Court of Appeals in November of that year and wasn't decided until it reached the U.S. Supreme Court the following spring, with the lower court decision being reversed after it was shown that the state legislatures in those states had "clearly articulated" their individual state policies, rendering Southern Motor Carriers "immune from antitrust liability."[161] On March 28, 1985, a headline in SMC's hometown *Atlanta Constitution* proclaimed "Supreme Court Upholds Joint Ratemaking" and the accompanying article by Calvin Lawrence, Jr., reported:

> "The U.S. Supreme Court, confirming the ability of states to regulate intrastate commerce, ruled Wednesday that state-approved price fixing is exempt from federal antitrust laws. The court voted 7-2 to reverse a federal appeals court decision that collective ratemaking by private motor carriers is illegal. The case was brought by the Atlanta-based Southern Motor Carriers Rate Conference and North Carolina Motor Carriers Association, which represent truckers in

several southeastern states. The ruling clears the way for competing truckers to meet and set rates subject to (continued) approval by state public service commissions. 'The court's ruling vindicates what we've been doing for 50 years,' said Jon Grant, a spokesman for the Georgia Public Service Commission. 'It's a system that works. For the shipping public, advantages include simplified tariffs and standardized rates,' he said."[162]

Respected Atlanta attorney Alan Hirsch of the Atlanta-based law firm Arnall Golden Gregory represented SMC and got the better of a Justice Department led by U.S. Attorney General Edwin Meese. Along the way, none other than Senator Edward Kennedy also got involved, when, as chairman of the Senate Transportation and Infrastructure Committee seven years earlier, he was responsible for federal agents coming to the SMC offices in Atlanta to search files and issue a subpoena for Farriba's appearance at a Kennedy-led, D.C.-hearing in May 1978. Apparently, nothing other than testimony ever came from that episode, but in looking back, Farriba remarked, "You better believe I was nervous. To this day I don't know if it had to do with deregulation in general, our case before the Supreme Court, or even the Teamsters (union involvement in the industry). I really had no idea what they were looking for."[163]

In *Trucking Country,* Hamilton makes note of the Kennedy episode as it related to the industry as a whole and even includes Ralph Nader among consumer advocates "who disagreed that government and labor intervention in trucking was 'ripping-off' the public's 'pocketbooks.' He also referenced the previously discussed "agricultural exemption" as a "template for deregulation" and maintained that's what really brought the Massachusetts senator into the fray, helping then-President Carter push it through Congress - that along with deregulation momentum and Teamster-busting.[164] But regardless, it was an experience Farriba would never forget. Later he even got a letter from Kennedy complimenting his forthright contribution to the proceedings, still an SMC³ keepsake.[165]

Chapter ten
"Intimidating Times"

John Bagileo has been a transportation attorney for five decades. A product of the old Interstate Commerce Commission's Honors Program, he began his career as a transportation clerk in 1966, and has dealt with the legalities of every issue the industry has faced since. No one was more aware of the changes facing motor freight when the ICC disbanded in favor of a new and, perhaps, less qualified governing agency, the Surface Transportation Board (STB), in 1996.

That would come only a year after Bagileo met Jack Middleton in 1995, when his Washington, D.C.-based practice was representing "all bureaus" or at least all that remained following the onset of deregulation over a decade earlier. "It had made them all very dependent on the larger carriers, the Roadways, ABFs, Con-ways, and Yellow Freights of the world. And like the bureaus, it was a very intimidating time for the smaller carriers," he acknowledged.[166]

Sensing the changes ahead and looking to take advantage of the opening of all routes throughout the country, the SMC Board, as usual one of the more proactive collectives on the trucking landscape, instructed Farriba, still executive vice president, to apply for a new concept, "nationwide authority." In fact, the Board's directive became one of the first orders of business on Bagileo's plate when he began working with SMC. "At that stage of his career, Vernon was not going to do something that would damage relationships with the other bureaus," Bagileo related. "He knew his friendships developed over years with the other bureau general managers would be damaged by SMC going against what had always been the system's regional mindset and he wasn't going to do it."

Fortunately for all parties involved, however, the leadership change at SMC was already in the works and Middleton didn't harbor any such reservations. Bagileo acknowledged, "That was the first order of business Jack and I began working on as soon as he took over in 1996 and officially hired me as general counsel."

Unlike the ICC, which had made it very difficult for carriers to obtain broader operating rights, "the floodgates seemed about to open under the STB." According to Bagileo, "The political climate of the mid 1990s was reflective of the shippers and their belief that the antitrust immunity enjoyed by the bureaus was a real thorn in their side and something they wanted to bring down."[167]

Coming as this did at the same time as the ramp-up in technology, another trend Farriba was only too glad to leave behind, the various bureaus were already "on guard" and becoming competitors rather than "sister bureaus" as had previously been the case. Middleton stated, "When we first applied for nationwide authority, I think Rocky Mountain actually flirted with joining us and Middlewest thought they could just wait and ride our coattails if we were successful."

In addition, Middleton indicated there was "a flight from the bureaus" taking place with larger carriers moving away from long-standing memberships in some, if not all. Over an 18-month period, he estimated SMC's revenue structure diminished by approximately $3 million in tariff sales and about $2.5 million in carrier dues.[168] A surge in interline agreements between carriers contributed to this development. Although sloppy at first and sometimes complex (with customers often billed in segments), these "pooling arrangements" became more common as bureau participation declined.[169]

Meanwhile, moving forward, their application for nationwide authority needed support from both shippers and carriers and needed to be proven beneficial to "the public interest." Cost and revenue had to be projected "throughout the scope of service" and nationwide needs "absolutely reflected." Bagileo said, "Shippers had no choice if carriers, acting independently, continued discounting practices because the bureaus had always served as carrier agents. The bureaus provided the shield that the carriers liked to hide behind when it suited them. In the case of class rates, federal statutes had to be justified."[170]

At a hearing in Washington at the STB offices in early 1996, "SMC submitted its application requesting nationwide collective ratemaking authority to serve its member motor carriers' expanded transportation and pricing needs," and Bagileo was "grilled by commissioners about why nationwide authority was necessary."[171] The executive director of NASSTRAC, the National Shipper's Strategic Transportation Council, actually surprised everyone by coming out in support of SMC attaining nationwide status, but the three STB commissioners were really the only ones that mattered "and I will always believe they had it in their minds that they were going to do away with the bureaus no matter what," Bagileo emphasized. "That hearing was just the first step."[172]

Except that for the next ten years no decision was forthcoming. "They just kept delaying action because they knew what they wanted, forcing us (SMC) to keep renewing our application (second application was in December 1996) and justifying our antitrust existence." At the same time, the other bureaus were watching and displaying more and more animosity towards SMC and its nationwide push. "By that time, all the bureaus were scurrying," Middleton noted. "With our merger, we were in better shape than most, but it was a new era with everybody trying to avoid debt and before long some of the other bureaus were involved in blocking our application."[173]

In 2000, SMC's application was refiled yet again. "That's when the greatest opposition from the other bureaus occurred," Bagileo remembered. "The head of Rocky Mountain even made an appearance before the STB to personally register opposition."[174] At the same time, two technology related lawsuits were initiated against SMC, one by Microsoft over an unauthorized use of software and the other by the Niagara Frontier Bureau (remember their pre-merger agreement with CSA) over "intellectual property infringement." Both provided temporary hindrances, but not much else and were settled out of court.[175]

Before that year was out, Congress also passed legislation that restricted bureaus from achieving nationwide authority, a drastic development that had Middleton and Bagileo scrambling for a way around that unexpected statute. Suddenly faced with the prospect of a protracted lobbying campaign (and from what they were told by several congressmen, it would take at least five years to reverse any law), the smile of good fortune never was brighter than the day they were introduced to Dawson Mathis, a former five-term Georgia congressman with all the right connections. "I think I can take care of that for you," he confidently told them after learning of their legislative plight. Fortnately for SMC, no truer words were ever spoken. In fact, access to the chairman of the House Transportation Appropriations Committee soon materialized and it wasn't long before Mathis was able to report back, "Consider it done."[176]

Unbelievable as it seemed, just 14 months after becoming law in October 2000, that legislation was suddenly reversed in December 2001 with the passing of an omnibus appropriations bill that included a legislative rider re-opening the nationwide authority issue to the everlasting benefit of SMC. "We couldn't believe our good fortune and how easily it had happened," Bagileo recalled. "It was an amazing experience, but one aided by our determination to not take no for an answer." Middleton added, "And then we spent the next five years rebuilding our case for nationwide authority."[177]

That was also about all the time that was left for collective ratemaking. On June 27, 2007, the STB finally got around to fulfilling its apparent, but unstated goal since replacing the ICC more than a decade before. That day, the STB Board announced its decision from a periodic review of the motor carrier bureaus. In its opening statement, it effectively "terminated all outstanding motor carrier bureau agreements." In doing so, it explained:

"The Board concluded that termination of these agreements was necessary to protect the public interest, particularly the public's interest in reasonable rates for shippers. The agency also found that antitrust immunity may be terminated without significant adverse effect on motor carrier efficiency or profitability or other policies favored under the motor transportation policy (previously) set forth. The agency stated that it would be incumbent upon the bureaus to determine the extent to which their present activities comply with the antitrust laws or would need to be reformed. To the extent the bureaus are uncertain about their exposure to antitrust liability; the Board encouraged them to consult advisors regarding the bounds of permissible activity and to take advantage of the business review procedure administered by the Antitrust Division of the United States Department of Justice. To provide time for the industry to adjust to a new environment without antitrust immunity for motor carrier activities, the Board provided that its decision would not become effective until September 4, 2007."[178]

Numerous petitions were filed seeking more adjustment time for what everyone in the industry suddenly realized was to be the absolute end of collective ratemaking, but there's no doubt the final nail in the coffin of bureau antitrust immunity was driven that summer day in 2007 by the STB – despite granting an additional four months. It wouldn't become effective until January 2008.[179]

In reality, however, there was no amount of extra time that could have preserved (much less brought back) the bureaus and collective ratemaking unless they were already positioned to be viable entities in what was a totally new environment without antitrust. And by 2007, there was only one well positioned to do so – Southern Motor Carriers, which by that time had been rechristened SMC^3. While Middlewest (as noted) would proceed to function in the same way (although at a far smaller market share) and at least one more would manage to continue (Pacific Inland in Portland, Oregon) in a reduced capacity as sales representative for SMC^3 on the West Coast, the others ceased operations.[180] As with so many other industries in the 21st Century, technology reigned and SMC^3 had become the most viable technology provider for motor freight pricing.

Meanwhile, in October of that year, *DC Velocity's* Peter Bradley wrote:

> "For less-than-truckload (LTL) shippers, 2007 has been a pretty good year. It's not just that they're enjoying more rate negotiating leverage than they've had in some time. It's also that they (have) received word of an important and long-sought legal victory that could open the way to more motor carrier rate competition. Assuming it withstands legal challenge (which it did), the ruling could have far-reaching effects on the industry, giving shippers greater influence in the system, stripping freight bureaus of collective ratemaking approval, and perhaps, smoothing the way for carriers and shippers to explore new and far less complex ways of pricing LTL freight."

Obviously, SMC^3 was not alone as a motor freight entity adapting to a new playing field where antitrust exemptions no longer applied.[181]

Chapter eleven
"Values Driven" Trilogy

Even before the days of antitrust immunity were officially over and the era of technology and data had completely taken hold, Southern Motor Carriers, under Middleton's watch, was already expanding its outreach. In fact, re-branding efforts in 2003 that were responsible for inserting the superscript three at the end of SMC had a very focused and compelling reason – the need to recognize a new concentration at SMC^3, education. It was added to technology and data to form a unique trilogy of service for the industry.

Middleton had long theorized that SMC^3, under his watch, would always be "values driven," and no greater example of his bend-over-backwards approach could be found than the client response rendered Estes Express when flooding basically shut down its Richmond headquarters in 2004 - or at least shut them down until SMC^3 (among others) came to the rescue in less than 24 hours.[182] According to Estes' own *Legacy of Service* brochure, the shutdown was the result of Tropical Storm Gaston, which dumped over a foot of rain on Central Virginia in just a few hours, resulting in "almost five feet of mud and water" on the ground floor of the "Big E's" main building, "shorting out all of the computer hardware and cutting off communications capabilities used in terminals and by customers around the country." Immediately, SMC^3 technicians were on call and on the job, both en route and on-site from both their Atlanta (what by that time had become suburban Peachtree City) and Louisville offices, and because of such instantaneous, "round-the-clock" service, little data was lost and everything was back on-line and operational within a week's time.[183]

That same value-based, customer service incentive was obvious when education was added to the SMC^3 mix along with technology and data. Already with a long history of hosting regular GRC meetings and more elaborate GRC gatherings at various southern resort towns, Middleton would take those kinds of annual events to another level after being profoundly inspired by what he heard at the retirement dinner of an industry leader in 1995. "As a young executive, I was captivated and touched by this retirement speech, especially the fact this man's greatest disappointment had been his inability to foster and improve communication and collaboration between carriers and shippers. It was something that resonated and remained on my mind," he continued. "When I became SMC^3 President and CEO, I decided to take up this torch and to try and make the difference I felt was so needed and important to our industry."

The vehicle he would use to accomplish this goal would become SMC^3's Industry & Educational Services group (I&ES). In his words:

> "With the purpose of developing two annual conferences filled with educational and purposeful industry and general content useful to both carriers and shippers. It would provide a forum for carriers and shippers to learn together; to network and collaborate in addition to celebrating quality social time together."[184]

Starting in 1996, both the winter and summer conferences were born. They would bring transportation leaders and experts from all segments of the supply chain to address representatives of attending companies from throughout North America on the subjects, trends, and most compelling concerns facing the industry, as well as the global, financial, and political issues currently making news. According to Middleton, the early years of his new concept were difficult with little enthusiasm or internal support amidst the many other concerns being faced by SMC^3. Aided only by his executive assistant, he had to schedule, plan, produce, and emcee the entire program, and it took several years to attract the kind of carrier and shipper interest that would finally gain support from his SMC³ management team. In addition, he took the unprecedented step of developing an associate membership program for shippers and logistics providers (3PLs), something that fit well with the educational component and would lead to increased participation in the years ahead.

  Once "the educational program had legs and SMC³ was growing and continued to reflect success," it became obvious to Middleton that he would need to concentrate his leadership efforts elsewhere. "It became apparent that I no longer had sufficient time to continue shepherding these programs, as much as I would have loved to do so, and knowing that a good friend and long-time industry executive, John Rader, was looking for a new opportunity, I contacted him with an invitation to meet and learn my vision in order to assess if it was a role he might like to assume moving forward," Middleton stated. "John and I spent a great deal of time together and he completely embraced my excitement and accepted our offer to become the first director of SMC³'s I&ES program in 2001."[185]

  A former SMC Board member who had held numerous positions throughout the industry during nearly 40 years in the business, Rader had experience in pricing, traffic, sales, operations, and marketing when he was approached by Middleton. From his start as a management trainee at Carolina Freight in Cherryville, North Carolina and stops at a series of transportation related destinations, including Sealand Services in New Orleans, Service Merchandise in Nashville, Averitt Express in Cookeville, Tennessee, Southeastern Freight Lines in Columbia, South Carolina, and Overnite in Richmond, Virginia, there wasn't too much that Rader hadn't been involved in when it came to moving freight. But it was a brief, two-year stint at Avon Products, where he added the shipper's perspective and a chance to be a part of putting on large conferences (some with over 400 attendees) that really prepared him for the I&ES trail he blazed.

"While I was vice president for pricing and traffic and later for marketing at Southeastern Freight Lines (1986-96), I had been part of the American Trucking Association Sales and Marketing Council that hosted annual educational conferences for its members. That was before it also became one of the committees the ATA had to do away with for cost-cutting reasons," Rader remembered. "Estes Express was one of the carriers that had real concerns about the loss of those conferences and one of several that became very excited about the possibility of SMC[3] picking that service up. Except for maybe a band and dancing at one social function, the former GRC meetings had been very tedious, boring, two-day affairs, even when held in a resort location. Transitioning them into well planned, multi-day conferences where the important trends and elements of the industry would be addressed by leaders and experts in the field was a stroke of genius on Jack's part. Attendees could take acquired information back to their individual companies that would benefit supply chains throughout the country and I got real excited about the prospect and the challenge."[186]

Actually, along with the twice-yearly, industry-as-a-whole conferences that Rader would be asked to plan, organize, and direct, he was also charged with hosting smaller annual meetings for two other industry-related groups, the Transportation Sales and Marketing Association or TSMA, and the claims managers of the various carriers, shippers, and other receivers of freight, who would gather for a Lost Prevention Conference known as LPC. Needless to say, this constituted a huge undertaking and responsibility in its earliest days and once committed to the job, 60-plus hour workweeks became Rader's norm in Peachtree City.[187]

His first year was largely as an observer, as Middleton continued to plan and run the five-year-old conferences prior to Rader officially taking the reins in 2002. At the same time, he recalled not being high on everyone's "most welcome list" as he set up his new shop within the organization. "There was some bumping of chests, so to speak. Marketing obviously didn't like me coming in and commandeering much of their time and budget, and I wasn't the most popular guy with leadership and Sales either, especially when I started making requests and asking favors for things that weren't previously part of most job descriptions. I was definitely the new kid on the block and for awhile, I think, I&ES was viewed as the stepchild. But thanks to Jack making sure everyone understood the importance we would play moving forward, the acceptance and buy-in eventually developed to the point of it becoming one of the most significant things the organization does."

Throughout this start-up and transition, Middleton displayed the confidence that Rader needed. "Jack showed great confidence in me and I needed that to have the determination it took to get everything done. I started to realize that everything I had done before in the industry, all the different components that I had experienced in all my previous stops, came together to help me focus on the program format, topics, trends, and speakers we needed to make the conferences successful. In the beginning, Jack's contacts in Washington at the Surface Transportation Board, Federal Motor Carrier Safety Administration, and other agencies were also critical to us coming up with the best curriculum possible and getting off to a good start. In those early days, he (Jack) leveraged a lot of relationships to ensure we started with the caliber of speakers and presentations that we wanted to become expected at any SMC^3 conference. Because of that, I think we established a level of excellence right off the bat that got the industry's attention and kept its people at every level coming back year after year."[188]

Admittedly nervous his first year in charge, especially while assuming master of ceremony duties along with everything else, Rader believes the biggest turning points on the conference road to success were the collective decision to come up with a theme for each meeting, beginning in 2003, and the securing of YRC Worldwide Chairman and CEO Bill Zollars as a presenter for both conferences in 2005. Rader said, "As a huge name in the industry, Bill's presence provided instant credibility and after speaking at our January conference, his anticipated return really set the stage for our biggest summer turnout up to that point. From the beginning, we felt our January conferences got us out ahead of possible competition and with people like Bill involved, it became obvious that participants who came to the winter meetings and liked what they got there were likely to come back for the same quality in a more family-friendly location each summer."[189]

Gradually, accolades began to come Rader's way – comments like "you sure run a good meeting" became commonplace. From an initial attendance of 85 for his maiden, 2002 winter conference, average numbers quickly reached 250 and above before his finale in January 2010. Along with carriers and shippers, logistics providers known as 3PLs (third party logistics) became more and more prevalent among the attendees.

The driving force, however, remained content. "We were always striving for bigger and better content," Rader advised. "I was constantly doing market research, reading all the trade publications, and getting referrals from key people over the phone, trying to validate key topics and speakers. We were constantly seeking the emerging topics that everyone was gravitating towards and any supply chain innovations on the horizon."[190]

At the same time, Middleton and the SMC^3 Board worked together to ensure the best locations for both winter and summer events. "After their site selection, we (I&ES) were brought back in to negotiate with what were always premier properties, the kind of places with all the bells and whistles that leave attendees impressed. I never for one minute doubted the capability of the places they chose to host a conference. I knew the level they aspired to would be the best," Rader acknowledged.

At the same time, all the meeting facilities, rooms, menus, décor, audiovisual, lighting, transportation, keynote, etc., etc., had to be checked and re-checked, as site visits were made and every detail considered in a constant, year-long cycle spent getting ready for each event. Gradually, entertainment became bigger and more diversified with quality acts, another Middleton requirement and one he would always have final say on. Even the spouses of attendees had special activities planned just for them, a seldom-found feature at other trade-based conferences and another means of keeping industry leadership coming back.[191]

Eventually, for lack of growth, the separate TSMA and LPC conferences were phased out, but industry seminars were added, an even better outgrowth of the new educational mission. After identifying "ongoing subject matter that could be taught on a recurring basis," LTL Seminars providing newcomer instruction on such things as "basic LTL operations, how a carrier determines a rate, and how to make things as profitable as possible for both shipper and carrier" were held on a regular basis in places like Atlanta, Boston, and Chicago. At the same time, a Contract Law Seminar (including how to write bilateral contracts, "treating both sides equally") and a Lost Prevention Seminar became "super participatory events," according to Rader. Held in Atlanta once a year, they averaged 50 to 100 participants from all over the country.[192]

Since Rader's retirement in 2010, the I&ES leadership duties have been assumed by Tom Swinson, whose in-house team has doubled while the conferences have grown to 400-plus no matter where they are held. Exclusive summer locations have included major cities like Chicago, San Diego, Las Vegas, and Boston, as well as more out-of-the-way resort destinations like Myrtle Beach, South Carolina; Coeur d'Alene, Idaho; and Naples, Florida.

"It's a constantly evolving mission. We are always looking for new ways, current topics, and the best speakers to better educate the supply chain," Swinson stated. "We want to help in the development of better managers and decision makers for the entire industry."[193]

Among the ways I&ES will be providing educational outreach in the future is through the virtual environment as well as the traditional. When asked to elaborate, Swinson said, "We are planning to use social media, webinars, smart talks, online blogs, and the repurposing of audiovisual files as just a few of the virtual means we have available. We even want to use those mechanisms in our seminars with the idea that the new virtual content will complement the traditional presentations we've always had. The one aspect that virtual attendees would miss is the networking that remains such a huge part of our conferences and something we never want to lose."

As transportation hub for the entire Southeast, Atlanta retains its appeal as home for SMC³'s annual winter conference, now known as Jump Start. "The largest portion of our membership and attendees remain in the Eastern U.S., so Atlanta still has a wealth of growth opportunities," Swinson said. Jump Start alone was expected to soon reach 500 participants.

At the same time, Connections, which has become the designated name for the more family-oriented summer conferences, will continue to take place in various locales from coast-to-coast. "It's the same, current supply chain content as Jump Start, but it offers the professionals in our industry a chance to involve their families at a more vacation-like setting," he confirmed. "We think the mix is what helps keep them both successful."[194]

Mix is also the word for how SMC³ hopes to grow its educational conferences - with railroad executives, port authority professionals, more and more shippers, and technology developers as just a few of the groups on their attendance radar along with the traditional carriers and more recent third party logistics providers, who currently compose the majority. Under Swinson's watch, conference content has also expanded to include such presenters as leaders of the Panama Canal, port authority officials, and warehousing and distribution experts, as well as a broader mix of economists, political analysts, and financial forecasters, all designed to foster better understanding of the national and international marketplace in which freight moves. "The bottom line is we've got to continue to evolve with the marketplace and adjust to the learning needs of the next generation of executives from all modes of transportation if we want to remain a key part of the SMC³ story," Swinson concluded.[195]

Chapter twelve
Of Rates and The Cloud

The final SMC³ General Rate Committee meeting was held on January 25, 2007, but long before that - before antitrust immunity was finally and irretrievably eliminated from collective ratemaking, benchmarking had become a lasting part of the motor freight costing process. Remember Bill Ball and Masco Industries demanding a benchmark as a major shipper in the late 1980s, an important, contributing factor in the promotion of the new motor freight technology then taking shape? Continuing that concept into the new century, a 2003 executive summary produced by SMC³ stated, "Industry benchmarking seeks to soften the impact of uncertainty through the creation of standards for measurement, reporting, and informed decision making."[196]

Such comments and the thought process behind them raised an important question or two for this story – the question of how motor freight rates are calculated. No history of a former collective ratemaking organization that survives to the present day, primarily as the result of providing rate-producing software for now and the foreseeable future, would seem complete without addressing this bottom line issue. How, indeed, are such things as time, distance, fuel, weight (or space), labor, insurance, security, maintenance, and damage (or loss), all obvious expense-producing factors, measured and combined in order to formulate an honest, competitive, and justifiable rate for shipping purposes?

A recent eHow online story offered an example of how truckload (TL) is based on a standard per-mile formula. In laymen's terms, it stated:

"1) Calculate the mileage between the starting and destination points. For this example, the trip begins in Atlanta and ends in Miami.

2) Divide the overall rate by the number of miles from the start to destination. The rate in this case is $3,100 and the mileage between Atlanta and Miami is 680 (3,100/680 = 4.56). The per-mile rate is $4.56.

3) Calculate the cost of transporting the load. On average, the truck gets 5.5 miles per gallon (of gas). The truck will use 123 gallons of diesel (fuel) for the 680-mile trip and $3 is the cost per gallon of diesel (123x3 = 369). The transportation cost is $369.

4) Multiply the truck driver's hourly rate by the length of time needed to complete the trip. The truck averages 60 miles per hour. The 680-mile trip will take about 11 hours (680/60 = 11.33). If the driver pay is $12 per hour, the cost for the driver is $132 (11x12 = 132).

5) Add the gas (fuel) cost and the truck driver pay ($369+$132 = $501).

6) Divide the total cost of the trip by the number of miles in the trip (501/680 = 73.7). Rounded up, the cost of the trip for the shipper is 74 cents per mile.

7) Subtract the per-mile cost of the trip from the per-mile rate to arrive at the per-mile profit of the trip for the carrier. ($4.56-$0.74 = $3.82). The per-mile profit is $3.82."[197]

Unfortunately, no such simple example is possible for the much more complicated LTL ratemaking. Instead, Acker, SMC³'s resident guru offered the following breakdown of factors in terms typical to any LTL pricing negotiation:

"Physical Pickup
Driving time from the terminal to the first stop and from the last stop back to the terminal known as stem time. The man minutes needed to drive from stop to stop known as variable running time. And the time spent at a customer's dock locating the shipment and its freight bill.

Terminal Issues
Any transfer of a shipment and its paperwork from a pickup vehicle to a linehaul vehicle, which is known as cross dock. Also, the time required to load the linehaul vehicle along with any repackaging or reorganizing of the shipment that is necessary for safe transport.

Linehaul Factors
The miles driven; the fuel consumed; equipment and maintenance depreciation; the allowance for circuity (indirect miles); the weight or volume of the freight, affecting how much a trailer can carry; and equipment utilization (exactly how full is that trailer?).

Breakbulk
Any movement of a shipment and its paperwork from an incoming linehaul vehicle that requires the loading of an outgoing linehaul vehicle.

Physical Delivery
The driving time from the terminal to the first stop and the last stop back to the terminal, which again is stem time. Also, the man minutes spent driving from stop to stop, more variable running time. And the time spent at the customer's dock needed to locate and unload the shipment and its freight bill onto the delivery dock.

Administrative Cost
The time spent in billing and collection, including the allocation of overhead.

Shipper Influenced Issues
These might include trailer drop-off; multiple shipments and the wait time necessary at drop-off and pickup locations; a cargo made up of palletized or loose articles; whether or not a shipment was pre-loaded, reducing or eliminating terminal handling; the overall density of the freight; was it delivered or picked up at the carrier's terminal; and was the freight bill pre-coded and/or electronic."[198]

These have always been items considered in the calculation of LTL costs. Knowledge of the process and its requirements remains critical to accurate allocation even when relying on modern ratemaking technology. As previously noted, the 2007 STB decision to finally do away with collective ratemaking antitrust immunity wasn't necessarily well received by many of the carrier companies since it also threatened the rate classifications established by the bureaus, the prospect of which gave "some truckers the jitters," according to the same October 2007 *DC Velocity* story mentioned earlier. In that story, Randy Mullett, then vice president of government relations for Con-way was quoted:

> "We would be worried about that going away. It is easier to price when comparing apples to apples, with everyone signing off on the same base classification. It is so embedded in everything, even in the way people price their products – the goods themselves. It would require some bold steps by industry leaders on our side (carriers) and the shipping side. "[199]

Not to worry. Almost a decade later, classification, and more specifically class rates, are "still in vogue" as part of the costing process. Not only are they utilized by the individual carriers independently, they are also still built into the (now) CzarLite family of software.[200]

And speaking of that product family, as recently as 2004 CzarLite could still be run on an IBM mainframe in addition to Windows-based (and even older DOS-based) personal computers. But according to SMC[3] Vice President for Product Development and IT Services, CIO David Knight, that all changed in 2005 when everything became web-based by taking up permanent residence "in The Cloud." Now a public network rather than a private network, one that originally relied on floppy disks and later CDs, Knight acknowledged the technology revolution that SMC[3] has undergone in the last decade. Customers now reach out to SMC[3] systems mostly through the internet, including via the transportation management solutions (TMS) employed by the nation's largest shippers. "It's still all about the data, but we've made a big investment in becoming not just a technology provider, but an infrastructure provider," Knight admitted. "We now have two primary data centers and two backup data centers, and we've added two new sections and doubled our IT staff in the last five years, including an application lifestyle group and an integration group. By managing everything internally, we offer a whole XL delivery platform. We're a hybrid, an association that serves an entire industry with a technology component. Security is priority No. 1 at the top of what we call our 'Iron Triangle' along with performance and availability."[201]

CzarLite program developments (in no defined order) have included CzarLite AS/400 (or iSeries), CzarLite HP-UX, CzarLite Linux, RateWare, CzarLite RFP for bids, server based CzarLite, ProRater 2000, BatchMark, FastClass, Priority1, CarrierConnect, CzarLite for e-Commerce, and CzarLite for shipper agreements. According to an SMC[3] catalog, the CzarLite data is still market-based, offering a price list derived from studies of pricing on a regional, inter-regional, national, and international basis, and providing access to "a single, common baseline from which to conduct business." By now, it's truly "ingrained" in the motor freight/transportation business.[202]

One sampling of promotional material from the early 2000s stated:

"From transportation pricing and data technology to development and support, SMC³ is recognized as the leading pricing and routing technology provider in the industry. All SMC³ software products and services are designed for flexibility and can be easily tailored to meet specific needs. SMC³ offers pricing and routing tools to keep carriers on the leading edge of technology. Carriers utilize the software for billing, freight auditing, and payment; classification lookups; and in negotiating agreements for interline shipments. SMC³ (also) offers shippers a variety of technology tools that aid in the carrier selection process."[203]

Contrast that with more simplified, present-day marketing, which features less specifics and carrier emphasis, and more industry-wide outreach. An example:

"Thousands of North American transportation professionals, from specialized, niche, regional, and most carriers to world-class shippers and logistic service providers turn to SMC³ solutions to make their best transportation choices."[204]

As always, or at least since the conversion to technology driven rates occurred, SMC³ licensing agreements remain value based. In other words, the bigger the company, chances are the greater and more frequent its technology use will be. So, for the most part, bigger companies generally have agreements that pay more than those of smaller, less frequent users. At the same time, Jack Brooks, who has worked for SMC³ in a variety of capacities since the early 1960s (a record-setting 51-plus years), has witnessed an increase in the complexity of agreements in recent times as the organization's inside sales representative. "It's a lot more drawn out process than it used to be," he said. "Some of the license agreements now can take up to a year to work through."

After stints as a mailroom clerk, tariff records clerk, tariff compiler, and tariff supervisor that added up to his first 30-something years, Brooks had to make a much more drastic change if he was to remain with the organization when it moved to Peachtree City and the new technology took over. In fact, he found himself under Slaton, the then relocated director of sales. "I had to do something else if I wanted to stay," he acknowledged. "There was some downsizing going on and after more than 30 years, I didn't want to change companies, so I moved to Sales Support and learned as much as I could about CzarLite." In addition, he extended his already long commute from the easternmost extent of Metro Atlanta to the southwest side, something a lot of SMC³ personnel did rather than relocate their homes. "I couldn't replace what I already had by selling and moving, so I've been spending at least three hours in the car every weekday ever since, but it's been worth it to stay with a good company that truly values its people. I've been blessed with SMC³," Brooks said.[205]

Chapter thirteen
New Age, New Leadership

The growing trends in transportation and logistics are constantly on the mind of Marquette University's Doug Fisher. Like the previously quoted John Langley of Penn State and other college professors who teach the modern supply chain at universities and colleges throughout the nation, Dr. Fisher sees academic interest in the industry on the rebound after a down period, interest-wise, in the 1980s and '90s.

"What I'm seeing with the internet and e-Commerce is the whole world of logistics making a comeback that is closely tied to inventory management," Fisher recently reported. "An increasing number of students are coming to us hoping they are at the right time to enter a field that is responding to changing needs and looking for new professionals who don't want to be tied to a desk job. Speed and reliability are becoming critical even though supply chains are getting longer and if you lose the convenience factor, chances are you've lost the customer. That's created a need for such things as integrated modes of transportation and well positioned distribution centers, just two examples of the modern blend of logistics that's making our curriculum and our classes more exciting."

Whether business to customer or supplier to buyer, the customer centric values of Amazon that now has the Walmarts, Targets, and others in catch-up mode are also driving the academic arena of which Fisher is a part. "Most undergrads don't know much about the supply chain when they first consider college, but once they hear about it and the internships we have available, their fascination takes hold, especially with the prospect of jobs at Amazon or in new distribution centers from coast-to-coast. You can sense their excitement. They can't help but see opportunities," he emphasized.[206]

With Middleton's retirement imminent (February 2016), SMC³ must look to new leadership to face this modern age of logistics and bridge the transportation gaps. No longer about just motor freight pricing, SMC³ will rely on incoming President Andrew Slusher to remain an industry "game-changer." Already focused on the competitive landscape, Slusher indicated he must first address what will extend the lives of SMC³'s current products; what it will take to maintain relevance in the marketplace; and the best way (or ways) to maintain leadership for change in the industry. "First and foremost, we've got to continue to create value for customers to ensure relevance," he said.[207]

This could involve finding a new niche or acquisition complementary to what SMC³ already does. Or how about the dimensional-based pricing question already endorsed by the rest of the world that is currently making inroads in the U.S. despite the reluctance of shippers and many LTL carriers, especially the smaller ones? Within Slusher's own organization, this reluctance was recently voiced by Brad Gregory, senior vice president of marketing and software alliances, in an article for *American Shipper* magazine. In it Gregory emphasized:

> "Why spend all this time and energy to come out in a neutral position? Shippers don't want to go through all this change (to dimensional pricing) unless they see a benefit. There's a certain amount of risk associated with change, so there has to be a balance. Among LTL carriers, competition looks at this differently. A handful (the larger ones who already have the technology) think it's a great idea, while the others may think it's an opportunity to take customers who don't want to change and keep them on the class-based system."[208]

It's just one of many industry issues SMC³ will continue to examine in its immediate future, as are new technology initiatives like trucking load boards, "enabling LTL service to become transactional rather than just contractual by allowing for a more flexible selection of freight," according to Slusher.[209]

Because of past experience with the airlines in addition to the trucking industry, Slusher is uniquely qualified to consider advancements of the former, an industry he estimates being 10 to 20 years ahead innovation-wise, and see if some of those concepts might now work for the latter. A finance major at the University of Missouri with an MBA from Texas Christian University (TCU), Slusher began his career with the Federal Reserve Bank in Dallas before spending seven years with American Airlines in their Pricing & Yield and Technology & Innovation Departments, and five more working with Sabre Holdings (now Sabre Solutions), what became Travelocity - one of the first technology based travel companies.[210]

He realizes that technology remains SMC³'s biggest opportunity, but also its biggest threat. "We've got to develop a new generation of leadership and a new generation of products that create value by simplifying and standardizing. Our core competencies are obviously data and software, but from here on, we've got to build whatever serves the industry's emerging needs and not just chase ideas that never materialize. Technology can take away from those that are not prepared to adapt rapidly to a changing landscape. We've got to see where things are going and understand them before simply applying technology to solve business problems without first adapting ourselves," he added.

A more analytical mindset will probably be required of SMC³ in the future. Even with a current team of seasoned veterans, Slusher believes at least some future personnel will need to come from "non-traditional places that offer fresh perspectives." In addition, future SMC³ Boards will undoubtedly include industry professionals from all modes and industry competencies rather than just the traditional LTL carrier base, a history-making trend already begun with the naming of Greg West of C. H. Robinson (a 3PL) in 2015. Slusher added, "We've always provided valuable service to the industry and I'm sure that mission will continue. At the same time, we will be looking for extensions to the SMC³ brand; for what's current; and at keeping our offerings as contemporary as possible in order to remain good stewards of logistics, the supply chain, and of course, motor freight, both now and in the future."[211]

In so doing, Slusher will be looking to continue the legacy so remarkably maintained by Vernon Farriba and so strategically developed by Jack Middleton for at least the next 80 years. Perhaps an outside observer and industry expert like Fisher offered the most appropriate perspective of what that legacy means when he emphatically stated, "Jack and those before him did one helluva job. They basically left other folks in the dust. There's no doubt the industry as a whole and especially motor freight is better today because of the contributions of SMC³."[212]

Postscript

Continuing its commitment to the industry, rest assured SMC³ will service the needs of transportation and logistics in the 21st Century. In addition to technology and data, its educational conferences will focus on the trends and issues facing providers, partners, and the public at large in the modern transportation marketplace.

Following are just a few of the thought-provoking comments made by industry experts on topics impacting the industry at Jump Start and Connections conferences between 2012 and 2015 via randomly selected excerpts from SMC³'s *Review* magazine.

On supply chain success:
"There are all kinds of supply chain disruptions happening all over the world every day and it's only going to become a bigger problem. It's not going away and how a company responds will be key to their overall success in the future. I firmly believe that companies that develop supply chain partnerships will differentiate themselves and improve their competitiveness in the transportation marketplace." – Kelly Marchese, principal with Deloitte Consulting

On density-based (dimensional) pricing:
"Density does not always accurately reflect the service demands that some products put on the carrier, but it is always important. Density is always the starting point when we assign classes for products. At the same time, classification provides a truer assessment of the freight and the costs associated with handling it." – Don Newell of the National Motor Freight Transportation Association Commodity Classification Standards Board

On global transportation:
"The big fear for global trade is congestion. Another is the aging population. At the same time we cannot ignore exports. They offer much faster growth." – Walter Kemmsies, economist for Moffat & Nichols

On the ongoing truck driver shortage:
"Why not target them earlier; in high school. You don't want dropouts driving trucks and if they go to college they're not going to be truck drivers." – Donald Ratajczak, economic forecaster for Georgia State University

On so-called "big data":
"We've got to use data to transform transportation and cash in. It can provide opportunities to increase sales, enhance driver safety, improve asset utilization, and drive costs down. Big data can provide much shorter cycles when it's properly leveraged. It should drive revenues." – Sundar Swaminathan, senior director of industry strategy at Oracle

On e-Commerce:
"Prices to the shipper eventually have to go up. Online retailing has been driven by free shipping. The data shows a very high percentage of online buyers abandon their shopping carts once they learn there's no free shipping. The online shopper has been spoiled by Amazon and others, but that's eventually going to stop." – Greg Smith, consultant at Tech Mahindra

On employee-driven values:
"We find a lot of value in the culture of our organization. I've seen us do it right and I've seen us do it wrong. This is what it comes down to: convincing people (staff) we love their ideas and want to celebrate their victories. That's the difference between good and great." – Rick DiMaio, vice president of distribution at Office Depot

On capacity concerns:
"Are we going to have an industry-led economy in the future rather than a consumer-led one, as it has been? In transportation, there's actually more capacity getting away from the industry than coming in and we need to change that." – David Ross, managing director of global transportation and logistics at Stifel

On workforce challenges:
"No matter what the industry, different locations will have higher demand and less supply for certain talent and jobs. Don't ever think that problems of job supply and demand are not spread across the entire United States." – Brian Butcher, vice president for strategy and growth at ADP

On technology:
"When you enable technology, every one of your customers has access and can take advantage, and your ability to tie networks together becomes very important to the data you need. Through dedicated integration groups, transportation management tools, business intelligence at your fingertips, and all types of reporting, search, and work flow actions, technology optimization can save millions." – Monica Wooden, CEO and co-founder of Mercury Gate International

On supply chain collaboration:
"When it comes to logistics, collaboration has been around for a while, but it was limited historically by a tendency to pass the buck. Now two or more suppliers are actively getting together to drive value and partnership is taking place up and down supply chains." – Jeff Shoemaker, group manager of transportation for the Clorox Company

On energy and fuel:
"The road to transportation fuel independence will be very long unless we reach energy independence, which looks closer than

you think. Net exports of diesel fuel are going up. We export one of every five barrels of diesel fuel we produce. At the same time, energy independence would have no immediate impact on bottom line costs." – Derek Andreoli, senior oil analyst for Mercator International

On exports:
"There are exciting new overseas opportunities: 95 percent of the world's consumers live outside the United States. American companies deserve every chance to succeed. They need a level playing field and transportation and logistics are key to building, buying, and moving products." – Francisco Sanchez, U.S. under secretary for international trade

On the intermodal collaboration:
"We feel like we are tapping only a small segment of the potential market so far (utilizing both railroads and motor freight) and we envision very predictable growth in this area." – David Marsh, chief of supply chain for Hub Group's Unyson Logistics and Hub Highway

Appendix one

Current Fast Facts about Semi-Trucks

1. Semi-trucks average 45,000 miles annually, but long distance semis are closer to 100,000.

2. One third of all modern semi-trucks are registered in three states, California, Florida, or Texas.

3. Sixty-eight percent of all American goods are delivered by semi-trucks.

4. As a group, semi-trucks average 6.5 miles per gallon on diesel fuel.

5. The maximum allowable weight of semi-trucks is 80,000 pounds spread over 18 wheels.

6. A Detroit-built diesel, 14.8 liter, six-cylinder engine weighs 2,880 pounds.

7. Freightliner now leads production of semi-trucks, about 190,000 annually.

8. Anti-lock brakes, a major breakthrough in semi-safety, were required as of 1997.

9. Despite the driver shortage, there are currently 3.2 million truck drivers in the U.S.

10. Altogether, American semi-trucks total about 140 billion miles each year.

Source: http://popularmechanics.com (accessed July 7, 2015)

Appendix two

Key U. S. Railroad Regulatory Legislation

1887 – Interstate Commerce Act created the ICC and forbid excessive charges, pools, rebates, and rate discrimination by the railroads.

1890 – Sherman Anti-Trust Act was designed to eliminate any combinations of restraint to interstate trade.

1903 – Elkins Act ended the common practice of rebates for "most valued customers."

1904 – Hepburn Act established "just and reasonable" maximum rates.

1976 – Railroad Revitalization & Reform Act was designed to permit more freedom to set rail rates.

1980 – Staggers Rail Act curtailed regional railroad bureaus and phased out general railroad rate increases.

Sources: http://auuuu.com, http://countrystudies.us, http://howstuffworks.com (accessed July 8, 2015)

Appendix three

Ten Present Day Motor Freight Takeaways

The continuing U. S. economic recovery is expected to fuel construction, always one of the largest and most important freight providers.

In addition, increased shipments of durable goods (such as heavy equipment and automobiles) are expected to drive demand for American transportation.

On the other hand, shipments of textiles and printed material will decline along with the need to restock those inventories.

Growth in motor freight along with recent carrier fleet reductions means tighter capacity for the immediate future.

Long-haul trucking is expected to face increasing competition from the railroads, which are more fuel efficient.

Carriers should be able to raise rates to offset higher costs, but their pricing power will not be strong enough to cause their net margins to widen significantly.

The increased proportion of products from overseas will focus much of the growth of motor freight in this country on U.S. port cities.

Looser credit implies that more carriers should be able to add to their fleets in the not-too- distant future.

Truck driver demographics, where average age is over 55, means a continuation of the current driver shortage and more pressure to raise wages and benefits.

Volatile fuel prices caused by instability in major oil-producing countries remain the industry's biggest wild card despite more fuel efficient trucks.

Source: Jeffrey Humphreys, "Keep On Trucking." *Georgia Trend,* November 2014.

Chapter notes

Chapter 1 – Shared Success Story

1) John Langley, Telephone Interview with the author (December 16, 2014).

2) Michael Belzer, *Sweatshops on Wheels*, p 25.

3) *Southern Motor Carriers Rate Conference Organizations & Activities* (brochure), pp 2-3.

4) A. D. Dial (Atlanta Chamber of Commerce), Letter to L. A. Raulerson (November 27, 1935).

5) Lybrand, Ross Bros. & Montgomery (CPAs), Incorporation Notification (May 31, 1936); and Michael David, "Best State to Incorporate," http://gimmelaw.com (accessed December 15, 2012).

6) "North Carolina Trucking Association," http://nctrucking.com (accessed May 17, 2015).

7) W. M. Miller, "History and Function of the Southern Motor Freight Carriers Association," Speech to Greenville Motor Carriers Rate Conference (January 15, 1964).

8) Ibid.

9) Ibid; and Southern Motor Carriers Rate Conference Organizations & Activities (brochure), pp 2-3.

10) James F. Filgas and L. L. Waters, *Yellow In Motion*, pp 183 and 248.

11) Ibid, p 183.

12) Danny Slaton, Interview with the author (February 10, 2015); and Charlie Owen, Interview with the author (March 23, 2015).

13) Vernon Farriba, Interview with the author (February 18, 2015).

14) Ibid, March 23, 2015.

15) John Bagileo and Jack Middleton, Interviews with the author (February 23, 2015).

Chapter 2 – How Trucking Kept 'em On The Farm

16) Shane Hamilton, *Trucking Country*, pp 14-24.

17) Sam M. Lewis and Joe Young, *How ya gonna Keep 'em Down on the Farm* (sheet music), 1919.

18) "History of the Trucking Industry in the United States," http://enwikipedia.org (accessed February 15, 2012); and Jeffery L. Rodengen, *The Legend of Con-Way*, p 12; and Shane Hamilton, *Trucking Country*, pp 44-51.

19) Michael Belzer, *Sweatshops on Wheels*, p 22.

20) Stan Holtzman, *Big Rigs*, pp 12, 107, and 31.

21) Shane Hamilton, *Trucking Country*, p 46.

22) Ibid, p 45; and "History of the Trucking Industry in the United States," http://enwikipedia.org (accessed February 15, 2012).

23) Michael Kazin, A Godly Hero, pp 25-28; and Shane Hamilton, *Trucking Country,* pp 14-15.

24) Ibid, pp 15-21; and Michael Hiltzik, *The New Deal*, pp 103-112.

25) Shane Hamilton, *Trucking Country*, pp 24-42.

26) Ibid, pp 43-44.

27) Estes Express Lines, *A Legacy of Service* (80th anniversary brochure), p 4; and Marvin Schwartz, *J. B. Hunt*, pp 1-3; and "History of the Trucking Industry in the United States," http://enwikipedia.org (accessed February 15, 2015).

28) Shane Hamilton, *Trucking Country*, pp 44-51.

29) Stan Holzman, Big Rigs, p 12; and Shane Hamilton, *Trucking Country,* pp 46 and 48.

30) James Filgas and L. L. Waters, *Yellow In Motion*, pp 3-4, 7, 49-50, and 69.

31) Shane Hamilton, *Trucking Country,* pp 8 and 45-48.

32) Ibid, pp 46-47.

33) Ibid, p 51.

34) Ibid, p 53; and Michael Belzer, *Sweatshops on Wheels*, pp 24-25, 64, and 203.

35) Vernon Farriba, Interview with the author (February 18, 2015); and Michael Belzer, *Sweatshops on Wheels*, p 64.

36) Ibid, p 25; and Z. L. Pearson, Jack Fraser, and Vernon Farriba, Interviews with the author (February 5, 8, and 18, 2015); and Shane Hamilton, *Trucking Country*, p 53.

37) Ibid, p 54.

38) Ibid.

39) Ibid, pp 56-57.

40) Ibid, pp 57-58.

41) Doris Kearns Goodwin, *The Bully Pulpit*, p 192.

Chapter 3 – Regulation and Collective Ratemaking

42) Tom Lewis, *Divided Highways,* p 21.

43) Michael Hiltzik, *The New Deal*, p 429.

44) Tom Lewis, *Divided Highways*, pp 21-22.

45) Ibid, pp 22-23.

46) Michael Hiltzik, *The New Deal*, p 421.

47) Michael Belzer, *Sweatshops on Wheels*, pp 60-61; and Michael Belzer, *Paying The Toll*, p 11; and *Webster's Seventh New Collegiate Dictionary*, p 902.

48) Michael Belzer, *Sweatshops on Wheels*, p 25; and William Tye, *Encouraging Cooperation Among Competitors*, p 1.

49) John Bagileo, Interview with the author (February 23, 2015); and James Filgas and L. L. Waters, *Yellow In Motion*, p 183.

50) Motor Carrier Ratemaking Study Commission, *Collective Ratemaking In The Trucking Industry*, p iii.

51) Vernon Farriba, Interview with the author (February 18, 2015).

52) "Southern Motor Carriers Rate Conference and Other ICC Approved Collective Rate Bureaus (map)," 1938.

53) Vernon Farriba, Interview with the author (February 18, 2015).

54) Z. L. Pearson, Telephone interview with the author (February 5, 2015).

55) Leo Ambruzzese, "Milne Truck Lines Closing Operations," *Journal of Commerce* (September 13, 1987); and Bill Ryan, "Remembering Garrett: Garrett Freight Lines would have been 100 this year," *Southeast Idaho Business Journal* (July 11, 2013).

56) Ron Adams, *The Long Haul*, pp 42, 104, and 140.

57) "UPS to Buy Overnite Trucking Firm," *Los Angeles Times* (May 17, 2005).

58) Shane Hamilton, *Trucking Country*, p 54.

59) Michael Belzer, *Sweatshops on Wheels*, p 15.

60) Jeffery Rodengen, *The Legend of Con-way*, p 55.

61) Ibid, p vi.

62) Ibid, pp 68-75.

63) Z. L. Pearson, Telephone interview with the author (February 5, 2015).

64) Vernon Farriba, Interview with the author (February 18, 2015).

65) Jack Fraser, Telephone interview with the author (February 8, 2015).

66) Z. L. Pearson, Telephone interview with the author (February 5, 2015).

Chapter 4 – Interstate Transformation

67) Tom Lewis, *Divided Highways*, p 85.

68) Ron Adams, *The Long Haul*, p 5.

69) Tom Lewis, *Divided Highways*, p 85.

70) Ibid, pp 98, 102, 104, and 119-120.

71) "Interstate Highway System," http://enwikipedia.org (accessed January 30, 2015).

72) Tom Lewis, *Divided Highways*, p 314.

73) Ibid, pp 286-287.

74) Ibid.

75) Ibid, p 202.

76) Ibid, pp 204, 16, and 202.

77) Ibid, p 15.

78) James Filgas and L. L. Waters, *Yellow In Motion*, p 161.

79) Tom Lewis, *Divided Highways,* p 314.

80) Grant M. Davis (ed.) *Collective Ratemaking In The Motor Carrier Industry,* p 153.

Chapter 5 – Looking Back at Bureau Days

81) Leajar Brooks, Interview with the author (December 13, 2014).

82) Ibid, Telephone interview with the author (February 20, 2015).

83) Ibid.

84) Bill Reed, Interviews with the author (January 19, and February 19, 2015).

85) Leajar Brooks, Telephone interview with the author (February 20, 2015).

86) Dean Stowers, Telephone interview with the author (April 15, 2015).

87) Leajar Brooks, Telephone interview with the author (February 20, 2015).

88) Ibid; and Vernon Farriba, Interview with the author (February 18, 2015).

89) Ibid.

Chapter 6 – Of Zip Codes and Benchmarks

90) Danny Slaton, Interview with the author (February 10, 2015).

91) Shane Hamilton, *Trucking Country*, p 11.

92) Herb Matthews, *Family Driven Since 1934*, p 33.

93) Patricia Cavanaugh, "ICC Moves Swiftly to Implement New Motor Carrier Act," *Transport Topics* (July 7, 1980).

94) Danny Slaton, Interview with the author (February 10, 2015).

95) John Womack, Telephone interview with the author (February 26, 2015).

96) Danny Slaton, Interview with the author (February 10, 2015).

97) Charlie Owen, Interview with the author (March 25, 2015).

98) Ibid.

99) Julie Beach, Interview with the author (March 25, 2015).

100) Charlie Owen, Interview with the author (March 25, 2015).

101) Danny Slaton, Interview with the author (February 10, 2015).

102) Ibid.

103) Ibid.

104) Charlie Owen, Interview with the author (March 25, 2015).

105) Danny Slaton, Interview with the author (February 10, 2015).

106) Charlie Owen and Julie Beach (Interviews with the author (March 25, 2015).

107) Danny Slaton, Interview with the author (February 10, 2015).

108) Danny Slaton, "Introducing CZAR-Lite (collateral sales piece)," 1987; and Danny Slaton, Letter to Russell Kanauss (December 31, 1987).

109) Danny Slaton, Interview with the author (February 10, 2015).

110) Jack Middleton, Interview with the author (May 1, 2015).

111) Danny Slaton, Interview with the author (February 10, 2015).

112) Vernon Farriba, Interviews with the author (January 20 and February 18, 2015).

Chapter 7 – Surviving Identity

113) John Womack, Telephone interview with the author (February 26, 2015).

114) Vernon Farriba, Interview with the author (February 18, 2015).

115) "UPS Freight to Buy Overnite Trucking Firm," *Los Angeles Times* (May 17, 2005); and Rob Estes, In contact with the author (April 10, 2015); and Ken Burroughs, In contact with the author (April 15, 2015).

116) Vernon Farriba, Interview with the author (February 18, 2015).

117) Ibid.

118) Ibid.

119) Ibid.

120 Harwood Cochrane, Resolution for Merger of Southern Motor Carriers Rate Conference and Central and Southern Tariff Association (January 29, 1975).

121) Vernon Farriba, Interview with the author (February 18, 2015).

122) Jack Middleton, Interview with the author (March 25, 2015).

123) Vernon Farriba, Interview with the author (February 18, 2015).

124) Ibid.

125) Ibid; and Jack Middleton, Interviews with the author (February 23 and March 25, 2015).

126) Vernon Farriba, Interview with the author (February 18, 2015); and Danny Slaton, Interview with the author (February 10, 2015).

127) Ibid.

128) Homer S. Carpenter, Letter to Vernon Farriba and John Womack (January 10, 1978).

129) Vernon Farriba, Interviews with the author (February 18 and March 23, 2015).

130) John Womack, Telephone interview with the author (February 26, 2015).

131) Vernon Farriba and Jack Middleton, Interviews with the author (February 18 and May 21, 2015).

132) Vernon Farriba and Jack Middleton, "Chronological Listing of Major Events Affecting SMCRC During the 1960s, '70s, '80s, and '90s" (updated May 1998).

133) "Rate Bureaus Merger Effective June 6," *Traffic World* (June 5, 1989).

134) Vernon Farriba, Interview with the author (March 23, 2015); and Central States Motor Freight Bureau Memorandum to All Member Carriers (February 4, 1993).

135) Jack Brooks, Interview with the author (April 23, 2015).

Chapter 8 – Labor Pains of Merger

136) Julie Beach, Interview with the author (March 25, 2015).

137) Charlie Owen, Interview with the author (March 25, 2015).

138) Ibid; and Julie Beach and Jack Middleton, Interviews with the author (March 25, 2015).

139) Ibid; and "Southern Motor Carriers Print Shop (auction announcement)" (March 1, 1990).

140) Charlie Owen, Interview with the author (March 25, 2015); and Vernon Farriba and Jack Middleton, "Chronological Listing of Major Events Affecting SMCRC During the 1960s, '70s, '80s, and '90s" (updated May 1998).

141) Jack Middleton, Interview with the author (March 25, 2015).

142) Julie Beach, Interview with the author (March 25, 2015).

143) Ibid; and Charlie Owen, Interview with the author (March 25, 2015).

144) Vernon Farriba, Jack Middleton, and Danny Slaton, Interviews with the author (February 18, March 25, and February 10, 2015).

145) Julie Beach, Interview with the author (March 25, 2015).

146) Jack Middleton, Interviews with the author (Marcy 25 and May 21, 2015).

147) Charlie Owen, Interview with the author (March 25, 2015).

148) Vernon Farriba, Letter in 1989 *Southern Motor Carriers Rate Conference* (annual report).

Chapter 9 – Regulation Reminiscing

149) Jerold B. Muskin, "The Physical Distribution Infrastructure," *Transportation Quarterly*, p. 132.

150) Michael Belzer, Sweatshops on Wheels, pp 3-4.

151) Ibid, pp 15-16.

152) Tommy Gammons, Telephone interview with the author (March 21, 2015).

153) Michael Belzer, *Sweatshops on Wheels*, pp 25-30, 39, and 41.

154) Fritz Kahn, "Prelude to Deregulation," *Traffic World* (June 1, 1992).

155) Dan Acker, Interview with the author (March 31, 2015).

156) John Maynard, "Do Trucks Need Ratemakers?" *Atlanta Constitution* (June 29, 1986).

157) Kurt Freedlund, "Deregulation: Who Really Benefits?" *Traffic World* (June 8, 1992).

158) Michael Belzer, *Sweatshops on Wheels*," pp 65-66.

159) Mark Solomon, "States: Deregulation's Last Frontier," *Traffic World* (October 26, 1992).

160) Kurt Freedlund, "Deregulation: Who Really Benefits?" *Traffic World* (June 8, 1992); and Michael Belzer, *Sweatshops on Wheels*, pp 57 and 66.

161) 471U.S.48 – Southern Motor Carriers Inc. v. United States, http://openjurist.org (accessed March 2, 2015).

162) Calvin Lawrence, Jr., "Supreme Court Upholds Joint Ratemaking," *Atlanta Constitution* (March 25, 1985).

163) Vernon Farriba, Interviews with the author (January 20, February 18, and March 23, 2015); and "Kennedy Turns To Truck Deregulation (by *New York Times*)," *Atlanta Constitution* (May 30, 1978).

164) Shane Hamilton, *Trucking Country*, pp 131 and 224-228.

165) Edward Kennedy, Letter to Vernon Farriba (April 6, 1978).

Chapter 10 – "Intimidating Times"

166) John Bagileo, Interview with the author (February 23, 2015).

167) Ibid.

168) Jack Middleton, Interview with the author (February 23, 2015).

169) John Bagileo, Interview with the author (February 23, 2015).

170) Ibid.

171) John Bagileo, "Before The Surface Transportation Board (application statement)," *Southern Motor Carriers Rate Conference* (December 19, 1996); and John Bagileo, Interview with the author (February 23, 2015).

172) Ibid.

173) Jack Middleton, Interview with the author (February 23, 2015).

174) John Bagileo, Interview with the author (February 23, 2015).

175) Jack Middleton, Interview with the author (February 23, 2015); and Jack Middleton, "SMC[3]'s Role in Motor Carrier History (New Employee Class)" (April 12, 2012).

176) Ibid; and John Bagileo and Jack Middleton, Interviews with the author (February 23, 2015).

177) Ibid; and *Congressional Record*, http://congress.gov (accessed June 30, 2015); and *The Library of Congress*, http://thomas.loc.gov (accessed July 1, 2015).

178) "Motor Carrier Bureaus – Periodic Review Procedure," Surface Transportation Board (June 28, 2007).

179) John Bagileo, Interview with the author (February 23, 2015).
180) Jack Middleton, E-mail interview with the author (May 1, 2015).
181) Peter Bradley, "A Brave New World of Pricing," *DC Velocity* (October 1, 2007).

Chapter 11 – "Values Driven" Trilogy
182) Jack Middleton, E-mail interview with the author (May 1, 2015).
183) Estes Express Lines, *A Legacy of Service* (80th anniversary brochure), pp 20-21.
184) Ibid.
185) John Rader, Interview with the author (April 1, 2015).
186) Ibid.
187) Ibid.
188) Ibid.
189) Ibid.
190) Ibid.
191) Thomas Swinson, Interview with the author (April 27, 2015).
192) Ibid.

Chapter 12 – Of Rates and The Cloud
193) "Proposed Docket Before the GRC as Docketed on December 13, 2006 (memorandum, January 25, 2007); and Danny Slaton, Interview with the author (February 10, 2015); and "Benchmark Pricing for a Stable LTL Economic Environment" (SMC^3 executive summary, July 2003).
194) Hunter Taylor, "How to Calculate Trucking Rates", http://ehow.com (accessed March 2, 2015).
195) Dan Acker, E-Mail interview with the author (April 21, 2015).
196) Peter Bradley, "A Brave New World of Pricing," *DC Velocity* (October 1, 2007).
197) Dan Acker, Interview with the author (March 31, 2015).
198) David Knight, Interview with the author (April 27, 2015).
199) "Technology Tools for Transportation (SMC^3 product catalog)," 2004.
200) Ibid, p 14.
201) "Overview," http://smc3.com (accessed December 2014).
202) Jack Brooks, Interview with the author (April 23, 2015).

Chapter 13 – New Age, New Leadership
203) Doug Fisher, Telephone interview with the author (April 23, 2015).
204) Andrew Slusher, Interview with the author (April 27, 2015).
205) Eric Johnson, "Density Lacks Gravity," *American Shipper* (June 2015).
206) Andrew Slusher, Interview with the author (April 27, 2015).
207) Doug Fisher, Telephone interview with the author (April 23, 2015).

Selected Bibliography

471U.S.48 – Southern Motor Carriers Inc. v. United States. Open Jurist, http://openjurist.org (accessed March 2, 2015).

Adams, Ron. *The Long Haul: America's Trucking Companies*. Hudson, WI: Iconografix, 2008.

Ambruzzese, Leo. "Milne Truck Lines Closing Operations. *Journal of Commerce* (September 13, 1987).

Annual Report. *Southern Motor Carriers Rate Conference*. Atlanta, GA: SMCRC Printing, 1989.

Application Statement. "Before The Surface Transportation Board," *Southern Motor Carriers Rate Conference* (December 19, 1996).

Auction Announcement. *Southern Motor Carriers Print Shop*. Louisville, KY: Rosen Systems, Inc. (March 1, 1990).

Badkar, Mamta and Rob Wile. "Here's The Reason Why the Trucking Industry is Running Out of Drivers." *Business Insider* (August 17, 2014).

Bagileo, John. Initial Statement before the Surface Transportation Board in Support of Application (April 21, 2004).

Belzer, Michael H. *Paying the Toll: Economic Deregulation of the Trucking Industry*. Washington, DC: Economic Policy Institute, 1994.

Belzer, Michael H. *Sweatshops on Wheels*: *Winners and Losers in Trucking Deregulation*. New York: Oxford Press, 2000.

Board Update. "SMC³'s Continued Exemption as a Trade Association Under 501 (c)(6) of the Internal Revenue Code," http://agg.com (accessed March 29, 2015).

Bradley, Peter. "A Brave New World of Pricing," *DC Velocity* (October 1, 2007).

Brochure. *A Legacy of Service: The History of Estes Express Lines* (80th anniversary). Richmond, VA: Estes-Express Lines, 2011.

Brochure. *Southern Motor Carriers Rate Conference: Organization & Activities*. Atlanta,   GA: SMCRC Printing, 1989.

Bureau Map. "Southern Motor Carriers Rate Conference & Other

ICC Approved Collective Rate Bureaus." Atlanta, GA: SMCRC Printing, 1938.

Carpenter, Homer S. Letter to Vernon Farriba, SMC, and John Womack, CSA (January 10, 1978).

"Carter Signs Historic Motor Carrier Act of 1980." *Transportation Topics* (July 7, 1980).

Catalog of Sale. Central & Southern MFTA (March 1, 1990).

Cavanaugh, Patricia. "ICC Moves Swiftly to Implement New Motor Carrier Act; Initiates Major Changes In Regulatory Policy." *Transport Topics* (July 7, 1980).

Cochrane, Harwood. Resolution for Merger of Southern Motor Carriers Rate Conference and Central and Southern Tariff Association. Atlanta, GA (January 29, 1975).

Collateral Sales Piece. "Introducing CZAR-Lite." Louisville, KY: CSA Print Shop, 1987.

David, Michael. "Best State to Incorporate." GimmieLaw, http://gimmielaw.com (accessed December 2010).

Davis, Grant M. *Collective Ratemaking In The Motor Carrier Industry: Implication to the American Public*. Danville, IL: The Interstate Printers & Publishers Inc., 1980.

Decision Document. "Motor Carrier Bureaus – Periodic Review Procedure," Surface Transportation Board (June 28, 2007).

Dial, A. D., Atlanta Chamber of Commerce. Letter to L. A. Raulerson (November 27, 1935).

Employee Handbook. *A Better Understanding of the Trucking Industry and the Role Played by SMCRC*. Atlanta, GA: SMCRC Printing, 1987.

Executive Summary. "Benchmark Pricing for a Stable LTL Economic Environment," SMC^3 (July 2003).

Farriba, Vernon and Jack Middleton. "Chronological Listing of Major Events Affecting SMCRC During the 1960s, '70s, '80s, and '90s" Atlanta, GA: SMC^3, updated May 1998.

Filgas, James F. and L. L. Waters. *Yellow In Motion: A History of Yellow Freight System, Incorporated*. Bloomington, IN: University of Indiana Press, 1967.

Freedlund, Kurt D. "Deregulation: Who Really Benefits." *Traffic World* (June 8, 1992).

Goodwin, Doris Kearns. *The Bully Pulpit: Theodore Roosevelt, William Howard Taft and the Golden Age of Journalism*. New York: Simon & Schuster, 2013.

Hamilton, Shane. *Trucking Country: The Road to America's Wal-Mart Economy.* Princeton, NJ: Princeton University Press, 2008.

Hiltzik, Michael. *The New Deal: A Modern History.* New York: Free Press, 2011.

"History of Trucking Industry." IRS, http://irs.gov/business (accessed February 15, 2012).

"History of the Trucking Industry in the United States." Wikipedia, http://enwikipedia.org (accessed February 15, 2012).

Holtzman, Stan. *Big Rigs: The Complete History of the American Semi Truck.* Stillwater, MN: Voyageur Press, 2001.

Incorporation Notification. Lybrand, Ross Bros. & Montgomery (CPA) *Southern Motor Carriers Rate Conference,* May 31, 1936.

Kahn, Fritz R. "Prelude to Deregulation," *Traffic World* (June 1, 1992).

Kazin, Michael. *A Godly Hero: The Life of William Jennings Bryan.* New York: Knopf, 2006.

Kennedy, Edward. Letter to Vernon Farriba (April 6, 1978).

"Kennedy Turns to Truck Deregulation (by *New York Times*)." *Atlanta Constitution* (reprinted May 30, 1978).

Lawrence, Calvin, Jr. "Supreme Court Upholds Joint Ratemaking," *Atlanta Constitution* (March 28, 1985).

Lewis, Sam M. and Joe Young. *How You Gonna Keep 'em Down on the Farm.* New York: Mills Music, 1919.

Lewis, Tom. *Divided Highways: Building the Interstate Highways, Transforming American Life.* Ithaca, NY: Cornell University Press, 2013.

Matthews, Herb. *Family Driven Since 1934: The Story of Benton Express.* Atlanta, GA: BEX Publishers, 2010.

Maynard, John. "Do Trucks Need Ratemakers?" *Atlanta Constitution* (June 29, 1982).

Memorandum. Central States Motor Freight Bureau to All Member Carriers. Notice of Merger – CMB & MWB – Members Right of Review (February 4, 1993).

Memorandum. General Rate Committee to SMC[3] Membership for Re-constitution of 2005 SMC[3] GRC (November 5, 2004).

Memorandum. SMC[3] to General Rate Committee Members and Alternates. "Proposed Docket Before the GRC as Docketed on December 13, 2006" (January 25, 2007).

Middleton, Jack. "SMC[3]'s Role in Motor Carrier History," Introduction to SMC[3] New Employee Class (April 12, 2012).

Miller, W. M. "History and Functions of the Southern Motor Carriers Rate Conference." Speech to Greenville Motor Freight Carriers Association, Greenville, SC (January 15, 1964).

Miller, W. M. "Southern Motor Carriers Rate Conference History and Functions." Presentation to Georgia State College School of Business. Atlanta, GA (March 23, 1964).

Minutes. Meeting of Board of Governors of SMCRC. Atlanta, GA (October 30, 1936).

Minutes. Meeting of General Rate Committee of SMCRC. Atlanta, GA (September 23-24, 1937).

Minutes. Meeting of General Rate Committee of SMCRC. Atlanta, GA (October 29-30, 1937).

Motor Carrier Ratemaking Study Commission, *Collective Ratemaking In The Trucking Industry* (June 1, 1983).

Muskin, Jerold B. "The Physical Distribution Infrastructure." *Transportation Quarterly* (January 1983).

Product Catalog. "Technology Tools for Transportation." Peachtree City, GA: SMC^3, 2004.

"Rate Bureaus Merger Effective on June 6." *Traffic World* (June 5, 1989).

Report to The President and The Congress of the United States. *Collective Ratemaking in the Trucking Industry.* Washington, DC: Motor Carrier Ratemaking Study Commission (June 1, 1983).

Rodengen, Jeffery L. *The Legend of Con-Way: A History of Service, Reliability, Innovation, and Growth.* Fort Lauderdale, FL: Write Stuff Enterprises, 2008.

Ryan, Bill. "Remembering Garrett: Garrett Freight Lines would have been 100 This Year." *Southeast Idaho Business Journal* (July 11, 2013).

Schwartz, Marvin. J. B. Hunt: *The Long Haul to Success.* Fayetteville, AR: University of Arkansas Press, 1992.

Slaton, Danny. *Introducing CZAR-Lite.* Louisville, KY: Central & Southern Print Shop, 1989.

Slaton, Danny. Letter to Russell Kanauss, Huber Corporation (December 31, 1987).

Solomon, Mark B. "States: Deregulation's Last Frontier." *Traffic World* (October 26, 1992).

"Tariff & Pricing Background." Atlas Van Lines, http://atlasvanlines.com (accessed May 17, 2015).

Taylor, Hunter. "How to Calculate Trucking Rates." eHow, http://ehow.com (accessed March 2, 2015).

"The History of Trucking Regulation Timeline." Blog4Truckers, http://cash4truckers.com (accessed October 31, 2011).

"UPS To Buy Overnite Trucking Firm (by Associated Press)." *Los Angeles Times* (May 17, 2005).

Watkins, Edgar, Jr. (SMCRC attorney). "Evolution of Carrier Regulation." Speech to Wilmington Traffic Club, Wilmington, Delaware (November 1, 1944).

Author Interviews and Contacts (with relation to subject)

Dan Acker (SMC[3] Senior Vice President) March 31 and April 21, 2015.

John Bagileo (SMC[3] General Council) February 23, 2015.

Julie Beech (SMC[3] retiree) March 25, 2015.

Jack Brooks (SMC[3] Sales Associate) April 23, 2015.

Leajar Brooks (SMC retiree) December 13, 2014, January 20, and February 20, 2015.

Ken Burroughs (SMC[3] Board Chairman) April 15, 2015.

Leonard Duggan (former New England Motor Rate Bureau GM) February 8, 2015.

Rob Estes (SMC[3] Board) April 10, 2015.

Vernon Farriba (SMC retiree and former Southern Motor Carriers Rate Conference GM) January 20, 2015, February 18, 2015, and March 23, 2015.

Doug Fisher (Professor and Director, Center for Supply Chain Management, Marquette University) April 23, 2015.

Jack Fraser (former New England Motor Freight Bureau GM) February 8, 2015.

Tommy Gammons (retired Yellow Freight driver) March 21, 2015.

Tommy Hodges (SMC[3] Board) January 21 and April 20, 2015.

Brent Holliday (SMC[3] Board) April 20, 2015.

Russell Garrett (SMC[3] Board) April 21, 2015.

Larry Kerr (SMC[3] Board) April 20, 2015.

David Knight (SMC[3] Senior Vice President & CIO) April 27, 2015.

John Langley (Professor of Supply Chain Management, Penn State University) December 16, 2014.

Jack Middleton (outgoing SMC[3] President and CEO) February 2, February 23, March 25, May 1, 2015, and August 12, 2015.

Charlie Owen (SMC retiree) March 25, 2015.

Z. L. Pearson (former Rocky Mountain Motor Tariff Bureau GM) February 5, 2015.

John Rader (SMC³ retiree) April 1, 2015.

Bill Reed (SMC³ Board Director Emeritus) January 19 and February 19, 2015.

Danny Slaton (SMC³ Senior Vice President & COO) February 10, 2015.

Andrew Slusher (SMC³ President) April 27, 2015.

Dean Stowers (SMC retiree) April 15, 2015.

Tom Swinson (SMC³ Director of Industry & Educational Services) April 27, 2015.

Paul Weaver (SMC³ Board Director Emeritus) March 28, 2015.

John Womack (former Central & Southern Rate Association GM) February 26, 2015.

Acknowledgements

Cover Design
Andrew Harmon

Assigned Photography
Hiran Apani
Lee Cathey
Michael Gibson

Editorial Assistance
Dan Acker
Jim Castallaw
Vernon Farriba
Sharon Harmon
Jack Middleton
Danny Slaton
Kevin Springer

Administrative Support
Sharon Harmon

Photo Contributions
Estes Express Lines
Yellow-Roadway Corporation

Cover Endorsements
Rob Estes
Doug Fisher
John Langley
Yossi Sheffi
Lynn Westmoreland

(Special Thanks to All of the Above)

Index

11th Circuit Court of Appeals, 64
3PL (third party logistics), viii, 75, 78, 91

A

Accounting, 5, 29, 32
Acker, Dan, 60, 61, 82, 107, 108, 113, 115
ADP, 95
Agricultural Adjustment Act, 8
Alabama, 2, 4, 33
Amazon, 89, 90, 94
American Airlines, 91
American Trucking Association (ADA), 11, 35, 76
Andreoli, Derek, 96
Ardmore, Pennsylvania, 7
Arkansas, 9, 112
Arnall Golden Gregory, 65
Asheville, North Carolina, 3
Atlanta Chamber of Commerce, 3, 101, 110
Atlanta, Georgia, v, 1, 4, 27, 28, 30, 32, 33, 43, 44, 45, 46, 47, 48, 51, 52, 53, 54, 55, 64, 65, 73, 79, 80, 82, 87, 109, 110, 112
Atlanta's High Museum of Art, 29
AT&T, v
Autobahn, 21
Autocar Company, 7
Averitt Express, 31, 75
Avon Products, 75

B

Bagileo, John, 67, 68, 69, 70, 101, 103, 107, 108, 109, 113
Ball, Bill, 40, 81
BatchMark, 85
Beach, Julie, 38, 40, 42, 51, 53, 54, 104, 105, 106
Blanco, Rafael, 37
Board of Governors, 33, 48
Bogart, Humphrey, 8

Boston, Massachusetts, 19, 79
Brooklyn, New York, 7
Brooks, Jack, 86, 87, 106, 107, 113
Brooks, Leajar, 27, 28, 29, 31, 33, 104, 113
Brotherhood of Teamsters, 11, 16
Brown Transport, 28
Brown, Bill, 5, 28, 29, 33, 44, 48
Brown, Glenn, 48
Bryan, William Jennings, 8, 111
Buffalo, New York, 37
Buford, Georgia, 27
Bureau of Public Roads, 13, 21
Burroughs, Ken, 105, 113
Butcher, Brian, 95

C
C. H. Robinson, 91
California, 63, 97
Canada, 17, 21
Carolina Freight, 75
CarrierConnect, 85
Carter, Jimmy, 35
Central and Southern Rate Association (CSA), 15, 37, 38, 39, 40, 41, 42, 43, 44, 45, 46, 47, 49, 51, 52, 60, 70, 110
Central States Motor Freight Bureau, 15, 36, 37, 44, 49, 51, 106, 111
Chase City, Virginia, 8
Cherryville, North Carolina, 75
Chesapeake Bay, 25
Chicago, Illinois, 4, 7, 37, 79
Clinton, DeWitt, 25
Clorox Company, 95
Cochrane, Harwood, 43, 44, 60, 105, 110
Coeur d'Alene, Idaho, 79
Colony Square Hotel (Atlanta), 47
Columbia, South Carolina, 75
Con-way, 17, 67, 84, 101, 103
Con-way Central Express, 17
Con-way Eastern Express, 17
Con-way Western Express, 17
Congress (U.S.), 10, 13, 14, 22, 62, 63, 65, 70, 107, 112
Connecticut Eastern Motor Freight Rate Conference, 15
Connections, 80, 93
Consolidated Freightways, 10, 17, 48
Continuous Traffic Studies (CTS), 37

Contract Law Seminar, 79
Cookeville, Tennessee, 75
Cost Department, 32
CSA Board, 44
CSA Computer Services Department, 38
CSA Research Department, 52
CSA Standing Rate Committee, 51
CSA Tariff Department, 38
CZAR, viii, 39, 40
CzarLite (CZAR-Lite), vi, 40, 41, 54, 61, 85, 87, 105, 110, 112

D
Dallas, Texas, v, 91
Darby, Larry, 61
Daytona Beach, Florida, 33
Deeming, Edwards, 37
Deloitte Consulting, 93
Denver, Colorado, 15
Detroit, Michigan, 40, 97
Diamond Reo, 7
DiMaio, Rick, 94
Docket Bulletin, 29, 30
Dough Boys, 8
Drexel University, 57
Duggan, Leonard, 113

E
e-Commerce, viii, 85, 89, 94
Eastern Central Association, 15
Eisenhower, Dwight ("Ike"), 21, 22, 25
Elizabethton, Kentucky, 37
Elkins Act, 98
Erie Canal, 25
Estes Express Lines ("Big E"), 9, 73, 76, 102, 108, 109
Estes, Rob, 105, 113
Estes, W. W., 8, 9
Europe, 7, 21

F
Farmers Alliance (or People's Party), 11
Farriba, Vernon, 1, 2, 5, 18, 19, 29, 33, 43, 44, 46, 47, 48, 49, 51, 52, 54, 55, 56, 65, 67, 68, 92, 101, 102, 103, 104, 105, 106, 107, 110, 111, 113
FastClass, 85

Federal Express, 63
Federal Highway Act, 22
Federal Motor Carrier Safety Administration, 77
Federal Reserve Bank, 91
Federal Express (FedEx), 63, 64
Fisher, Doug, 89, 92, 108, 113
Florida, 2, 3, 4, 27, 32, 43, 55, 97
Fraser, Jack, 19, 102, 103, 113
Freightliner, 17, 97

G
Gammons, Tommy, 58, 106, 113
Garrett Freight Lines, 15, 16, 103, 112
Garrett, Russell, 113
Gatlinburg, Tennessee, 33
General Rate Committee (GRC), 18, 30, 33, 41, 60, 74, 76, 81, 111, 112
Georgia, 2, 4, 33, 64, 70
Georgia State University, 28, 94
Germany, 21
GRC, 18, 30, 41, 60, 74, 76, 108, 111
GRC Meeting, 18, 30, 41, 60, 74, 76
Great Depression, 8, 13
Great Lakes, 22
Gregory, Brad, 90

H
Hepburn Act, 98
Highway Revenue Act, 22
Hirsch, Alan, 65
Hodges, Tommy, 113
Holiday, Brent, 113
Honors Program - ICC, 67
House Transportation Appropriations Committee (U.S.), 70
HP-UX, 85
Hub Group Knyson Logistics, 96
Hunt, Johnnie Bryan, 9

I
IBM, v, 37, 39, 85
IBT, 11, 16
ICC, 3, 4, 10, 11, 13, 14, 15, 18, 19, 31, 32, 35, 37, 47, 49, 58, 59, 60, 64, 67, 68, 70, 98, 103, 104, 110
Idaho, 15, 79
Illinois, 36

Illinois Commerce Commission, 62
Indiana, 36, 54
Indiana University, 35
Indianapolis, Indiana, 35
Industry & Educational Services Group (I&ES), 74, 75, 77, 78, 79
Interstate Commerce Act, 98
Interstate Commerce Commission, 3, 4, 10, 67
Interstate Highway System, vii, 21, 25, 103
Interstates, 22, 23
Iron Triangle, 85

J
J. B. Hunt, 9, 102, 112
Jacksonville, Florida, 43
Jump Start, 80, 93
Just-In-Time Production, 23
Justice Department (U.S.), 65

K
Kansas City, Missouri, 49
Kemmsies, Walter, 94
Kennedy, Edward, 65, 107, 111
Kerr, Larry, 113
Knight, David, 85, 108, 113

L
Lance, Bert, 35
Langley, John, 1, 89, 101, 113
LaRue, Lash, 28
Las Vegas, Nevada, 79
Legal Department, 32
Linux, 85
Lost Prevention Conference (LPC), 76, 79
Lost Prevention Seminar, 79
Louisiana, 2
Louisville, Kentucky, 4, 36, 38, 39, 46, 47, 51, 52, 53, 54, 55, 73, 109, 110, 112
LTL (less-than-truckload), viii, 24, 30, 33, 35, 41, 42, 43, 58, 59, 60, 61, 72, 79, 82, 84, 90, 91, 108

M
Mack Brothers Company, 7, 9
Mailroom, 28, 30
Maine, 22

Maintenance, 32, 81, 83
Maislin decision, 60
Mann, Lester, 29
Marchese, Kelly, 93
Marquette University, 89, 112
Mars, 49
Marsh, David, 96
Masco Industries, 40, 81
Massachusetts, 65
Mathis, Dawson, 70
MCA, 13, 14, 16, 36
Meese, Edwin, 65
Mercator International, 96
Mercury Gate International, 95
Mexico, 21
Miami, Florida, 82
Michigan, 36
Microsoft, 69
Middle Atlantic Conference, 15, 49
Middleton, Jack, vii, 1, 2, 5, 19, 28, 29, 32, 33, 41, 45, 51, 52, 54, 55, 56, 67, 68, 69, 70, 73, 74, 75, 76, 77, 78, 90, 92, 101, 105, 106, 107, 108, 110, 111, 113
Middlewest Motor Freight Bureau, 15, 49, 68, 71
W. M. (Mike) Miller, 3, 33, 35, 101, 112
Milne Truck Lines, Inc., 15, 103, 109
Miracle on Ice, 35
Mississippi, 2, 4, 33, 64
Mississippi River, 3
Moffat & Nichols, 94
Motor Carrier Act of 1935, 2, 10
Motor Carrier Act of 1980, 35, 63, 110
Motor Carrier Ratemaking Commission, 61
Myrtle Beach, South Carolina, 79

N
Nader, Ralph, 65
Naples, Florida, 79
Nashville, Tennessee, 30
National Grange, 11
National Motor Freight Transportation Association Commodity Classification Standards Board, 93
National Recovery Administration (NRA), 13
National Shipper's Strategic Transportation Council (NASSTRAC), 69
New England Motor Rate Bureau, 15, 19, 113

New Jersey, 22
New Orleans, Louisiana, 75
New Penn, 16
Newell, Don, 93
Niagara Frontier Tariff Bureau, 15
North America, 74
North Carolina, 2, 3, 4, 33, 64
North Carolina Truck Owners Association, 3

O

O'Brien, Raymond, 17
Office Depot, 94
Ohio, 36
Ohio River, 3, 54
Oklahoma City, Oklahoma, 9
Old Dominion Freight, 16, 31
Oracle, 94
Overnite Transportation, 16, 43, 60, 75, 103, 105, 113
Owen, Charlie, 36, 37, 38, 39, 42, 51, 52, 53, 55, 101, 104, 105, 106, 113

P

Pacific Inland Tariff Bureau, 15, 72
Panama Canal, 80
Paris, France, 7
Peachtree City, Georgia, v, 73, 76, 87, 112
Peachtree Street (Atlanta), 29
Pearson, Z. L., 15, 17, 19, 102, 103, 114
Penn State University, 1, 113
Penn-Yan Express, 17
Pennsylvania, 22
Pocatello, Idaho, 15
Pope, Tony, 48
Portland, Oregon, 72
Potomac River, 3, 25
Pricing & Yield, 91
ProRater 2000, 85
Public Works Administration (PWA), 13

R

Rader, John, 75, 76, 77, 78, 79, 108, 114
Raft, George, 8
Railroad Revitalization & Reform Act, 98
Ratajczak, Donald, 94
Rate Department, 31

RateWare, 85
Reconstruction Finance Administration (RFA), 13
Reed-Bulwinkle Act, 14
Research Department, 27, 51
Richmond, Virginia, 43, 73, 75
Roadway Express, 10, 16, 24, 48, 67
Rocky Mountain Motor Tariff Bureau, 15, 19, 114
Roosevelt, Franklin Delano (FDR), 13, 21
Ross, David, 95
Ryder Truck Lines, 43

S
Sabre Holdings, 91
Sales Support Department, 87
San Diego, California, 79
Sanchez, Francisco, 96
Savannah, Georgia, 33
Sealand Services, 75
Sherman Antitrust Act, 64
Shoemaker, Jeff, 95
Shumate, John, 33
Slaton, Danny, 35, 36, 38, 39, 40, 41, 42, 46, 54, 87, 101, 104, 105, 106, 108, 112, 114
Slusher, Andrew, viii, 90, 91, 92, 108, 114
(as) SMCRC (or SMC), v, 23, 28, 29, 30, 32, 33, 34, 42, 43, 44, 45, 46, 47, 48, 49, 51, 53, 54, 57, 60, 64, 65, 67, 68, 69, 70, 73, 75, 106, 110, 112, 113, 114
SMC Board, 46, 47, 48, 67, 75
(as) SMC^3, v, vi, vii, viii, 1, 2, 5, 34, 38, 46, 49, 64, 65, 71, 72, 73, 74, 75, 76, 77, 80, 81, 82, 85, 86, 87, 90, 91, 92, 93, 107, 108, 109, 110, 111, 112, 113, 114
SMC^3 Board, vii, 78, 91, 113
Smith, Greg, 94
South, 3, 30, 31, 44
South Carolina, 2, 3, 4, 33, 75, 79
South-East Section, 31
South-Southwest Section, 31
Southeast, 29, 36, 42, 80
Southeastern Freight Lines, 75, 76
(as) Southern Motor Carriers Rate Conference, v, 3, 4, 5, 16, 19, 27, 28, 43, 45, 48, 64, 71, 73, 103, 105, 106, 107, 109, 110, 111, 112, 113
Special Executive Committee, 44, 45
Spring Street (Atlanta), 28,29
St. George, Utah, 15

Staggers Rail Act, 98
Standing Rate Committee (SCR), 18, 29, 61
STB, 67, 68, 69, 70, 71, 84
STB Board, 70
Stifel, 95
Stowers, Dean, 31, 104, 114
Supreme Court (U.S.), 60, 64, 65, 107, 111
Surface Transportation Board, 67, 77, 107, 109, 110
Sutton, Evelyn, 28
Swaminathan, Sundar, 94
Swinson, Tom, 79, 80, 108, 114

T

Target, 89
Tariff Department, 31, 33, 38
Teamsters, 11, 16, 35, 65
Tech Mahindra, 94
Technology & Innovation, 91
Tennessee, 2, 4, 33, 64
Tennessee Mafia, 30
Texas, 97
Texas Christian University (TCU), 91
Textile Section, 31
The Beltway, v
The Perimeter, v
The Tom Landry Freeway, v
They Drive By Night, 8
TL (truckload), viii, 24, 58, 59, 81
Traffic Division — Masco, 40
Transportation Sales and Marketing Association (TSMA), 76
Travelocity, 91
Tropical Storm Gaston, 73
TRS-80, 39
Truman, Harry, 14
Tulsa, Oklahoma, 9

U

U. S. Department of Agriculture (USDA), 9
United Parcel Service (UPS), 43
United States, 2, 17, 21, 31, 62, 64, 95, 96, 102, 107, 109, 111
University of Missouri, 91
UPS, 63, 103, 113
UPS Freight, 16, 43, 105

V
Virginia, 2, 4, 8, 33

W
Walmart, 89
Washington, D.C., 19, 25, 32, 47, 67
Washington, George, 25
Watkins Motor Lines, 55
Weaver, Paul, 55, 114
Webb Wallace Estes, 8
West Coast, 15, 72
West, Gene, 48
West, Greg, 91
Western Mountain Rate Bureau, 15
Windows, 42, 55, 85
Wooten, Monica, 95
Womack, John, 36, 39, 44, 45, 46, 47, 48, 104, 105, 110, 114
Works Progress Administration (WPA), 13
World War I, 7, 9
World War II, 21

Y
Yellow Freight, 9, 10, 16, 24, 35, 48, 58, 67, 113
YRC, 9, 16, 24, 77

Z
Zollars, Bill, 77